SAINTS ALIVE!

Enid Broderick Fisher

Fount

An Imprint of HarperCollinsPublishers

Fount Paperbacks is an Imprint of
HarperCollins*Religious*
Part of HarperCollins*Publishers*
77–85 Fulham Palace Road, London W6 8JB

First published in Great Britain
in 1995 by Fount Paperbacks

3   5   7   9   10   8   6   4   2

Copyright © 1995 Quartz Editorial Services
112 Station Road, Edgeware HA8 7AQ

Enid Broderick Fisher asserts the moral right to be
identified as the author of this work

A catalogue record for this book is
available from the British Library

ISBN 0 00 627 894–9

Printed and bound in Great Britain

The author and copyright-holders gratefully acknowledge the kind
co-operation and advice of Father Thomas Allan of Westminster
Cathedral, London, and the Rev. Keith Newton of the Church of
St Anne and the Holy Nativity, Knowle, Bristol.

CONTENTS

INTRODUCTION

I F you are accustomed to thinking that patron saints are confined to representing countries – St George for England, St Patrick for Ireland, and so on – and one or two aspects of daily life – nearly everybody knows that St Christopher is patron saint of travellers, for example – then this book will be a revelation to you. Through these pages, we introduce you to a considerable number of those who, down the ages, have been adopted as patron saints for all sorts of professions, as well as health problems and many other features of daily life.

Most saints led extraordinary lives, packed with enough incidents to fill several lifetimes. Many, you will find, turned to Christ early and encountered the most powerful temptations – even seductions – to lure them away from their chosen path. Early saints, from Roman times, often also suffered the most gruesome deaths for their faith – tortures so grisly that it is hard to believe the human mind could think them up. These tortures were frequently ordered by enraged pagans who had failed to win them over in any other way.

Some started out living the good life to the full – wearing rich clothes, eating vast meals and living in sumptuous palaces – before giving it all up for a life of poverty and prayer. Others were veritable sinners – soldiers who took a delight in persecuting Christians, gamblers, or even thieves – until, suddenly, they 'saw the light' and converted to Christianity. Still more drove themselves into an early grave doing good for those less fortunate than themselves. In fact, every saint you will read about here has a unique life story.

ORIGINS OF SAINTHOOD

So how did the very idea of sainthood come about? The early Christian Church was quick to recognise that there were people whose lives and faith would earn them an exalted place in Heaven. According to Scripture, the prayers of a holy man are deemed more beneficial than those of ordinary mortals and, as traditional doctrine teaches that the Church of God exists in Heaven as well as on Earth, early Christians began the practice of invoking these exemplary men and women for support when praying to God. These devotions continue to be observed in the Eastern Orthodox and Roman Catholic Churches, while attitudes towards saints vary among the many sects which constitute the Protestant Church, from the higher churches within the Church of England, which also venerate saints, to the lower churches and non-conformist religions, such as Methodism, where the stand on sainthood is simple recognition of New Testament saints, with no veneration.

The first saints were usually martyrs, or the immediate Apostles of Christ, or both; and veneration – regarding a saint with deep respect and reverence in recognition of his or her holy state – first began in the second century in local communities, at the place of a saint's tomb. Then, as Christianity spread to lands further and further afield, veneration of these saints was introduced by missionaries. Some saints achieved world-wide status this way; while others, not thus trumpeted, remained significant only in their immediate village community.

Details of their lives, much in demand, were furnished either by first-hand accounts – the *Acts of the Apostles* in the New Testament, largely written by the Apostle Luke, is one example – or by later writings from stories handed down from generation to generation. Lists were also drawn up of saints recognised by the fledgling Christian Church – the early Roman martyrologies (compiled by the Christian Church in Rome), for instance. Later, this thirst for information produced accounts where just one or two facts were embellished with a full life story, and many of these were set down in *The Golden Legend* of James of Voragine, Archbishop of Genoa, who died in 1298, and similar collections of lives of the saints.

As the centuries progressed, so did reasons for sainthood. Martyrdom was no longer the principal qualification. Others included an exemplary life; demonstrable holiness; good works; the founding of religious houses; exposure to visions; and miracles reported after a saint had been invoked, say, to cure an illness or to help avert a war.

In the early Christian period, sainthood was conferred on an individual by popular acclaim. However, as time went on, the Church deemed it more appropriate that a formal procedure should be entered into – canonisation. This, literally, means the saint's name is incorporated into the Canon, or list, of saints approved by the Church. The process began under the auspices of Pope Celestine III in the 12th century and, within 100 years, under Pope Gregory IX, papal approval, after intensive investigation, became the only legitimate means of canonisation.

However, there are no living saints. They are nominated after death, when convincing arguments are put forward to the Pope in Rome. Some saints will have shown sufficient worthiness to their contemporaries to be nominated by them soon after their death, and canonisation follows relatively quickly. Others remain unsung for centuries, until someone studying their case feels them worthy of recognition and gathers evidence to support a belated nomination. A famous, modern example is the canonisation of the Forty Martyrs of England and Wales, who died for their faith in the 15th-17th centuries, but who were not recognised as saints until 1970.

TEST OF WORTHINESS

The procedure from exemplary person to saint is complicated and drawn out. First, the nominators have to produce evidence of worthiness. Originally, this was tested in what resembled a courtroom battle, with the Pope as judge. While the nominators argued the case for sainthood, a disinterested party, often one of the Pope's staff, argued against, producing what evidence he could to dispute the claim. The purpose of this was to test the worthiness of the candidate. Because this opponent, in so doing, was trying to deny the candidate his exalted place in Heaven, he was called the Devil's Advocate. Nowadays, the evidence is presented to the Congregation for the Causes of Saints, a committee of Cardinals and other Church officials, who weigh the nominators' claims against the counter-claims of the Devil's Advocate and send their recommendations to the Pope, who pronounces on the individual's worthiness for sainthood.

Once past this test, however, the candidate is still not home and dry. First, evidence of a miracle must be proved. Saints, it should be understood, do not work miracles themselves; rather, they act as communicators of the wonder from God to the recipient. Thus, a miracle is said to occur with the inexplicable curing of a terminal disease in a sufferer who has prayed to the saint for intercession. Once the existence of one miracle is accepted, the candidate is beatified, and endowed with the prefix 'Blessed'. Sainthood follows if three miracles can be proved.

Once a petition for canonisation is accepted, a service is held in St Peter's Church, Rome, with the Pope officiating, in the presence of cardinals and all interested parties – for example, nominators and witnesses. A Feast Day is assigned to a saint at the time of canonisation, and is usually the day of death or martyrdom or, put another way, the first day of his or her life in Heaven – *Natalis* – but the Feast Day could also be the day when relics were moved to a place of worship. Consequently, some days boast only one saint, while others are packed out. Of course, not all saints are venerated in all countries, so it is unlikely that a worshipper would be spoilt for choice.

In this book, we have named Feast Days assigned by the Western (Roman Catholic) Christian Church but, often, the Eastern Orthodox Church will have chosen different days on which to honour saints in common, usually early saints.

You will probably be familiar with a handful of Feast Days already, without really having to think about it – St Stephen on 26 December (Boxing Day), St Valentine on 14 February, St Swithin on 15 July and the Eve of All Hallows (Saints) on 31 October (Hallowe'en), are examples which spring readily to mind. As far as the Church is concerned, celebrations are simple and straightforward. A Mass is said in honour of the saint, and perhaps an icon is decorated, but the Church does not issue hard and fast rules as to how the rest of us might celebrate, only that whatever we do should have some religious aspect.

WHICH PATRON SAINT?

Assignment of patronage to a profession, way of life or to guard against illness is decided by the Pope, but not necessarily the one who accepted the nomination for sainthood. Indeed, centuries can pass before the association is recognised and given official sanction; and, sometimes, patronage evolves through custom and practice, without official recognition at all.

The choice of saint to represent a country is made by a reigning monarch, government or Church leaders. A petition for approval is then sent to the Congregation for Causes of Saints in the Vatican. If devotion, in that country, to the saint in question can be proved to the Congregation's satisfaction, approval is given via an Apostolic Letter from the reigning Pope.

Many countries adopt a national hero, as in the case of Sweden's saint, Eric the Martyr, or France's Joan of Arc. Some choose a local bishop or clergyman, who may have been martyred – the Czech Republic's John Nepomucen, 14th-century Vicar-General of Prague, was thrown into a river – or a dedicated person who has helped others less fortunate than himself, such as Peru's Peter Claver, renowned for his ministry to slaves. Others opt for a saint who best represents a country's hopes and aspirations. A well-known example is St George, adopted for England by King Richard the Lionheart during the Crusades in the 12th century.

Many Christian countries, and sometimes countries of a different state religion but with a vigorous Christian community, choose the Blessed Virgin Mary as patron saint. As the Mother of God – affirmed by the Church at the Council of Ephesus in the fifth century – Mary is universally recognised as having a special place in Heaven, while Roman Catholic and Eastern Orthodox faiths venerate her as the first among the saints. In 1944, Pope Pius XII dedicated the entire human race to Mary. She has at least six Feast Days, and the countries who have chosen her as patron celebrate one of these dates, on which a signal event in her life took place.

Most important are the Immaculate Conception (8 December), which does not refer to the Virgin birth as is often supposed, but to Mary's freedom from Original Sin at her own birth – otherwise, according to Church doctrine, only Jesus was born in this perfect state; her Birthday (8 September); the Annunciation – when the Archangel Gabriel told her she would give birth to the Son of God (25 March); the Visitation – when Mary visited her kinswoman Elizabeth, the mother of John the Baptist (31 May); and the Assumption – when Mary was bodily assumed into Heaven at her death (15 August).

Patronage may also be ascribed to the name of a shrine to the Blessed Virgin Mary, usually in a place where a vision has occurred. Mexico's patron, Our Lady of Guadaloupe, where she appeared, as a Mexican woman, to a young boy on a hill outside Mexico City, is one such example. Elsewhere, Mary is venerated under one of her many names, on a date when she was invoked in an hour of crisis.

Over the centuries, literally thousands of saints have been recognised and, every so often, the Church has a shake-up, to rationalise the numbers. Those with slender qualifications, those who may not have existed except in legend, or those too obscure to have any real claim, are not derecognised as saints, but their veneration is discouraged, and their Feast Days suppressed.

But the saints are not just the preserve of those arms of the Christian Church which retain devotion to them. Many people who have never seen the inside of a church still feel that saints have some mysterious power. As you read through this book, you will discover just how many are linked to our work, our health, our everyday activities, and even the lands in which we live.

THE WORLD
OF WORK

YOU may be surprised to learn that your occupation – whether it be a profession or a trade
– is likely to boast a specific saint who can be invoked to intercede on your behalf. The accounts
in this chapter tell fascinating stories behind the
choice. Perhaps the saint, during his or her lifetime,
followed the same occupation, or a particular incident brought him or her into contact with it. A saint
may even have been martyred – that is, put to death
purely because he or she was a Christian – in a
particular way that makes a connection with a
particular occupation. (One example is Apollonia,
patron saint of dentists, who suffered torture by
having her teeth smashed by her Roman persecutors.) Whatever the connection, these intriguing
tales give each saint a special relationship with a
particular livelihood. Through this, each is believed
by many to be in the best position to intercede for
help from God if problems arise.

ACCOUNTANTS

Matthew

Saint day: 21 September

MATTHEW was perhaps the most controversial of the twelve men Jesus chose to be his disciples. Certainly, the choice attracted a lot of criticism, for Matthew was a publican, or tax collector. Such a man was about as popular then as he is now. He himself recounts that tax collectors and sinners were regarded as being one and the same. Even worse, however, he worked for the Romans, and the money he collected went straight to the hated oppressors.

Nevertheless, Matthew proved a worthy follower of Christ, keeping what meagre finances the disciples had under strict control. His preoccupation with figures and his chosen line of work made him the obvious choice to look out for the welfare of accountants. He has been represented in pictures and stained-glass windows down the ages accompanied by money bags or collecting boxes. In the Middle

Ages, he even appeared with spectacles, the better to pore over his account books.

Matthew wrote the first of the four Gospels in his old age, before being martyred for his faith – legend has it, in Ethiopia. His relics are said to have been brought from there to Brittany, France.

• Matthew is also patron saint of Book-keepers, Tax collectors and Customs officials.

ACTORS

Genesius

Saint day: 25 August

No one is quite sure when Genesius was born, nor even when he was canonised. But ever since mediaeval times, he has been recognised as patron saint of the stage. An intriguing legend explains how this may have come about.

At the request of the anti-Christian Emperor Diocletian, a special cabaret was to be performed in Rome, and the star of the show was, of course, Genesius, widely noted for a ready wit and an extensive comic repertoire. At one particular point, Genesius was to lie down on the stage and pretend to be ill, exclaiming to the other players that he wished to be delivered from sin before death and to be born again through baptism – a statement clearly intended to cause laughter by way of response from an audience of non-believers.

What actually happened, however, was to startle everyone present – including Genesius himself, not until then a man of faith: for we are told that as the 'fake' baptism was performed, Genesius saw a host of angels and proclaimed conversion to the true religion.

The emperor immediately ordered that he be punished with his life for false beliefs. But Genesius is said not to have sought pardon: instead, he declared again his faith, only regretting that he came to it so late in life.

ADVERTISING EXECUTIVES

Bernardino of Siena

Saint day: 20 May

BERNARDINO knew he wanted to spread the message of Christ from an early age. He was born in Massa, just outside Siena, Italy, in 1380, the son of the city governor. Orphaned by the age of seven, he was brought up by an aunt until old enough to enter a Franciscan order. The training was long and hard; and he remained cloistered for 12 years until 1417, when he began to preach the word, first in Milan and then all over Italy. Bernardino travelled everywhere on foot, delivering several sermons, of three to four hours apiece, each day. His style attracted large crowds, and he used all means available to bring them to Christ. He made them laugh, reduced them to tears, and drove home his message by storytelling, acting, and some good, old-fashioned denunciation.

He may even have been the first to use a logo. At the end of each sermon, Bernardino would brandish a plaque inscribed with the letters *IHS*, meaning Jesus. He became known for it, and cardmakers he had ruined, by denouncing gambling, recouped their losses by mass-producing plaques to hand out to the crowds.

After a spell as vicar-general to the Strict Observant branch of his Order, Bernardino felt the call of the open road and resumed his preaching. He was well past 60 and now needed a donkey to get him about. Early in 1444, he delivered 50 sermons in as many days in his home town, sensing it was his last visit. He died on 20 May in Aquila, while on his way to Naples.

Bernardino's perfection of the art of persuasion brought converts in their thousands. Small wonder the advertising industry looks to him for inspiration.

• Bernardino is also patron saint of Public relations officers and Hoarseness.

AIR HOSTESSES

Bona

Saint day: 29 May

BONA knew from a very early age that she wanted to spend her life on pilgrimages to shrines and burial places of saints and martyrs. It is this perpetual travelling that has made her the guiding light for air hostesses and, indeed, all air travellers, whether passengers or crew.

Bona was born in Pisa, Italy, in about 1156, and was brought up by her mother after her father died when she was a baby. Bona was still young when she started to have visions, urging her to travel to Jerusalem. As soon as she could persuade her mother to let her go, Bona embarked on the first of her many pilgrimages.

On her way back to Pisa, however, she encountered a hermit who suggested she convert the Saracens, as she was passing through their country. Bona set about her task with fervour but failed miserably, and was even thrown into jail. This experience did not dim Bona's resolve to travel, and she visited many shrines all over Italy, including St Peter's in Rome. She died of natural causes in 1207, at the age of 51.

Apprentices

John Bosco

Saint day: 31 January

JOHN Bosco spent his whole life teaching a trade to working-class boys who otherwise would have lived a life of destitution. Born in the Kingdom of Piedmont, now in Italy, in 1815, he was the youngest son of a peasant farmer who died when John was only two. He and his mother lived in extreme poverty until he became a priest in 1841. He made his life's work the education of disadvantaged boys and, at one stage, lived in poverty with 40 of them, teaching shoemaking and tailoring. His work grew until he had 150 boys in residence and a further 500 children in attached workshops where they were taught a wide variety of trades.

He was renowned not only as an eloquent preacher, but also for his gift of handling difficult youths without resorting to punishment. He founded the Salesian Order of Fathers, specifically to spread his work with boys; and by the time of his death in 1888, he had established 64 schools worldwide. A similar Order of nuns was founded to bring John Bosco's education ideals to girls. His schools now number many thousands, all over Europe and the United States, and are still engaged in teaching young people a trade.

ARCHAEOLOGISTS

Damasus

Saint day: 11 December

D AMASUS was born in Rome in 304. His father was a priest, and he became deacon in his father's church. His service to Christianity over the next 60 years was rewarded in 366 when he was elected Pope. Not all the clergy agreed with the choice, however, some having voted in an opponent; and it took the backing of the Roman emperor to secure the tenancy of St Peter's throne for Damasus. At that time, the Christian church was fragmented, and different branches had their own version of the Bible. When the Roman Emperor proclaimed the Roman Church to be the true Church which all others should join, Damasus took it upon himself to standardise the Bible so all could worship alike. Thereafter, his 'Vulgate' Bible was to be used throughout the Christian world for over a thousand years.

It was because of his spare-time activities of looking after the relics of Roman martyrs and ordering the drainage and opening up of the Roman catacombs which criss-crossed underneath the city that Damasus became the patron saint of archaeologists. Like his modern-day counterparts, Damasus labelled everything carefully, although usually with a poem or epitaph rather than a description and number. He died in 384, aged 80.

• Archaeologists also have Jerome as their patron saint.

ARCHITECTS

Thomas the Apostle

Saint day: 21 December

THOMAS is probably best known for his refusal to believe, on the say-so of the other apostles, that Christ had risen. He would only be convinced if he saw Jesus with his own eyes and touched for himself the wounds that killed his Lord. 'Doubting Thomas' has thus entered the language as a description of someone to whom only seeing is believing.

It is widely accepted that he voyaged to India to spread Christ's message, and was killed there by a spear in the year 72. Some say his body lies to this day at Mylapore, near to where he fell. Others insist his bones were moved to Italy. Either way, his supposed graves were soon adopted as shrines, and he became the subject of several books, such as the *Acts of Thomas*, written in the 2nd and 4th centuries by members of sects, such as the Gnostics.

How Thomas became the guiding light of architects is the stuff of legend. In these writings, Thomas is said to have told an Indian king that, as a builder by trade, he could construct for him a sumptuous palace. However, he spent the money he was given to complete the task on the poor, explaining to the enraged king that the palace he wanted would be his in Heaven as a reward for Thomas' good works. The king did not think much of this excuse, and was preparing to put Thomas to death when his brother died, went to Heaven, saw the palace and returned to confirm Thomas' story. Instead of killing Thomas, the king received baptism from him, as did his brother and many of his subjects. As a result of this legend, Thomas is often represented in mediaeval art with a builder's T-square in his hand.

• Thomas is the patron saint of Blindness, India and Pakistan, too. Architects, meanwhile, also have Barbara as their patron saint.

ARMS DEALERS

Adrian Nicomedia

Saint day: 8 September

ADRIAN was a Roman soldier in the personal service of the Emperor Diocletian, at the turn of the 4th century. Although a pagan, he had married a Christian wife, Natalia. Given his master's resolve to cleanse the Empire of Christians by the most ruthless persecutions, Adrian probably kept this to himself and masked his tolerance by guarding well those Christians who had been rounded up and who were destined for torture and subsequently death.

At one preliminary mass beating of 23 Christians, however, Adrian was so taken aback by their submission to their fate that he declared his conversion on the spot. Unsurprisingly, he was thrown into prison when

Diocletian got to hear of it. Natalia, Adrian's wife of only 13 months, disguised herself as a man and was able to enter his dungeon and give him food and clothing.

When Diocletian ordered his execution by dismemberment, Natalia was at her husband's side, and managed to retrieve a hand. Adrian's remains were cast on the fire, but a sudden storm put out the flames and fellow Christians took what was left of him for burial in Constantinople. Natalia went with the remains, and lived close by their burial place for the rest of her life.

Adrian is depicted in mediaeval art either accompanied by a sword, signifying his life as a soldier, or with an anvil, over which he was stretched prior to dismemberment – or both. It is the two emblems together that have suggested Adrian as patron saint of arms dealers.

• Adrian is also patron saint of Prison guards and Butchers.

ARTISTS

Luke

Saint day: 18 October

CURIOUSLY, it was Luke's way with words rather than his expertise with a paintbrush that should have made him eligible to be a patron saint. Long regarded as the most lyrical Gospel writer, his moving accounts of the parables are held up as perfect examples of verbal artistry. The legend that he made icons of the

Virgin Mary probably accounts for his adoption as mentor for artists, but in fact there is no proof he ever did. Nevertheless, Flemish works of the 15th and 16th centuries depicted him painting Mary, while earlier artists showed him in the process of writing.

Luke was undoubtedly a gifted writer, penning the *Acts of the Apostles* – often from first-hand knowledge. A Greek by birth, he trained as a doctor before accompanying St Paul on his journeys throughout Asia Minor. He was imprisoned with Paul and was responsible for preserving the health of the apostle.

It is not known when he died, but Constantinople and Padua, Italy, both lay claim to be his last resting place.

• Luke is also the patron saint of Doctors and Butchers.

Astronauts

Joseph of Cupertino

Saint day: 18 September

JOSEPH was born in 1603, the son of a poor carpenter in Cupertino, Italy. He began life as a bit of a no-hoper – poor, uninterested in holding down a job, and inept at one when he got it. He did, however, commit himself to Christ and, by sheer persistence and a lot of good luck, became a priest in 1628.

Thereafter, he led a life of simplicity and was an exemplary member of the clergy, healing the sick and devoting himself to prayer and contemplation. He stopped short of perfection, however, for he had a seeming inability to stop himself levitating, which irritated his masters so much that they packed him off to obscure monasteries where no one would see him. Nevertheless, he did attract a following, and gained many conversions, before he died, aged 60, in 1663.

His feats were truly remarkable. In all, seventy witnessed events of levitation took place. His most spectacular was lifting a 36-foot high cross, hitherto immovable by 10 burly workmen, through the air and setting it in place 'as if it were straw'. It takes no imagination to see why astronauts look to him for inspiration.

• Joseph is also the patron saint of Flying and Examinations.

BAKERS

Honoratus of Amiens

Saint day: 16 May

HONORATUS was Bishop of Amiens, France, at the end of the 6th century. He was born in the nearby village of Port-le-Grand, but nothing more is known of him until, as bishop, he received the relics of the saints Fuscianus, Victoricus and Gentian, which had been lost for 300 years.

He died in 600, and by 1060, cures were attributed to him. Several churches were dedicated to Honoratus, as were religious houses and, for reasons which are not apparent, he became venerated as the patron saint of all

men and women whose work brings them into contact with flour, particularly bakers, and especially in France. He is generally depicted in art with tools of the baker's trade.

BANKERS

Bernardino of Feltres

Saint day: 28 September

BERNARDINO was born Martin Tomitani in the state of Venice in 1439. His family was wealthy and he received a good education. He was a clever boy – at 12, he could write Latin verses, and his mother had to force him out to play. He studied law at the University of Padua; but when he heard a Franciscan friar preaching in the city in 1456, Martin decided to join the Order and was admitted as a novice the same year. He took the name Bernardino after the saint from Siena.

Although sincere in his views, Bernardino was terrified of preaching: he would freeze in the pulpit and his words dried up as he tried to speak. He prayed for fluency, and one day threw away his prepared notes and spoke from the heart. From then on, his preaching filled churches and thronged market places.

One vice which particularly bothered him was moneylending, where high rates of interest were charged even to the poorest who had no hope of paying it back. So when a monk set up a system whereby the poor could borrow at a low rate of interest for a small pledge, Bernardino threw his weight behind the venture, later adapting the idea to establish simple lending houses. His vision of institutionalising loans for the ordinary person has made Bernardino the guiding light of the banking business.

BEEKEEPERS

Bernard of Clairvaux

Saint day: 20 August

BERNARD was born near Dijon, France, in 1090, into a degree of wealth that promised an easy life, without much risk of ever having to work for a living. But by the age of 22, he began to yearn for a contemplative life. He set his sights on a run-down Cistercian foundation at Citeaux, and persuaded 31 companions, including some of his brothers, to join him.

This influx of new blood revived the fortunes of the Cistercian Order and so, in 1115, Bernard and 12 followers founded their own House in a place so inhospitable that it was known locally as the Valley of Wormwood. At first, Bernard imposed a harsh régime on his companions – coarse barley bread and boiled leaves for meals, when they were served at all, and severe punishment for the slightest infraction of the House rules – causing them unnecessary suffering. Fortunately, Bernard was not entirely blind to their distress, and he subsequently raised the standard of living, although the life remained one of grinding poverty. Many more devout men joined the Order and, over the next 40 years, over 500 Houses were established all over Europe, including 68 monasteries, such as Rivaulx in England and Mellifont in Ireland.

For a recluse, Bernard was not shy in coming forward to speak out passionately on matters of great importance to the Church, such as supporting the legitimately elected Pope, Innocent II, against a competitor, in 1130. He also railed against what he perceived as heresies so eloquently that many alternative thinkers were brought round to his view. His gentle but firm way of arguing converted the most ardent of opponents without a murmur. Indeed, he was nick-named 'Doctor Mellifluous', for the honeyed tones in which he conducted his arguments.

Bernard died in 1153, and was canonized just over 20 years later. His emblem in art is a beehive, representing his eloquence and sweet manner, and it is this which has marked him out as patron saint of beekeepers, and also the associated trade of wax melters.

• Bernard is patron saint of Gibraltar, too.

BOOKTRADE

John of God

Saint day: 8 March

A s a mercenary soldier who practised no religion, John of God seems, at first, an unlikely candidate for sainthood. Born in Portugal in 1495, he saw active service fighting for Spain as far away as Hungary. He then spent many years as a shepherd and did not become a committed Christian until he was 40.

He then decided to devote his life to the poor and oppressed, and planned to go to North Africa to rescue

Christian slaves. Although prepared to die in the attempt, friends warned him off, and John got only as far as Gibraltar. There, he became a pedlar, selling sacred books and pictures.

He made such a success of this that he travelled back to Spain and opened a bookshop in Granada. His prosperity was shortlived, however, as madness took hold of him. He gave away his stock of books, and was confined to hospital.

By 1539, John was cured, and went on to spend the remaining 11 years of his life tending the sick and ministering to the poor. He died on the altar steps in his chapel, suffering from the after-effects of rescuing a drowning man in a flood.

After his death, his followers formed the Brothers Hospitallers in his memory, and he became the patron saint of booksellers and printers, in memory of his early days on the road in Gibraltar.

BOOKSELLER.

BREWERS

Amand, Bishop

Saint day: 6 February

A MAND was born in Lower Poitou, northern France, in 584. At the age of 20, he decided to lead a contemplative life, and retired to a small monastery on the obscure island of Yeu, just off the coast. His father took a dim view of Amand's decision, and came after him, searching for over a year and then begging, pleading and threatening Amand with disinheritance.

Eventually, Amand left the island, as his father ordered, but did not return to Poitou. Instead, he travelled

to Tours, where he was ordained as a priest. He then moved to Bourges, where he stayed 15 years. After a pilgrimage to Rome, he returned to France and accepted the appointment as a roving bishop, in 629. Amand's mission was to convert, particularly in Belgium.

At first, the people were very hostile, and Amand was beaten up and thrown into a river on more than one occasion. In the end, he got through to them, and many were baptised. He also founded a nunnery at Nivelles, and monasteries at Ghent and at Elnon.

Amand was adopted as patron saint of brewers because of his missions in Belgium's prime beer-brewing territory. This patronage now extends to anyone connected with the alcohol trade.

• Brewers also have as patron saint Wenceslaus the Martyr.

BUILDING TRADE

Stephen

Saint day: 26 December

STEPHEN is universally accepted as the first Christian martyr. He came into contact with the Apostles at the very beginning of their ministry. He and six others were made responsible for distributing alms, leaving the Apostles free to preach. An educated man who spoke Greek, he soon drew attention to himself by his skilfully reasoned arguments that the coming of Jesus had changed forever our perception of God.

The Jewish priests took exception to this, arrested him and conducted a show trial. He was stoned to death in the year 34. These instruments of his martyrdom account for his selection as the champion of building workers.

• Builders also have Vincent Ferrer as their patron saint.

BUSINESS PEOPLE

Homobonus

Saint day: 13 November

HOMOBONUS – the name means 'good man' in Latin – was the son of a merchant in Cremona, Italy, who entered the family tailoring business. He was a devout man, and was known for his great generosity, especially to the poor. On 13 November 1197, while praying in church, he suddenly stretched out his arms in the form of the cross, fell flat on his face and died.

He was never a priest, nor the founder of a religious order, nor a martyr, but his good works earned him sainthood only two years after his death. His success as a merchant makes him an ideal role model for the business world, especially anyone connected with the cloth trade, through which he made the fortune that he chose to give to the poor.

• Merchants also have Nicholas of Bari as their patron saint.

BUTCHERS

Luke

Saint day: 18 October

LUKE originally trained in medicine; and ironically, in many ways, his expertise in the field of early surgery is probably at least partly responsible for his adoption as patron for butchers.

In Biblical times, and still in some religions today, butchers were not only purveyors of meat but also ritual slaughterers of animals. The methods used were in strict accordance with religious law. Certainly, this also had a lot to do with hygiene, in times when preservation was unknown except for salting, and diseases from deteriorating meat could kill.

The butcher, therefore, had to exercise a skill with a precision equal to that of the finest surgeon. There is no actual evidence that Luke himself was trained in this way, but his expertise in surgery gave him much in common with cutters of meat.

• Luke is patron saint of Artists and Doctors, too; while Butchers also have as patron saint Adrian Nicomedia.

CARPENTERS

Joseph

Saint day: 19 March

JOSEPH is the obvious choice of patron saint for carpenters, for it was he who taught Jesus Christ his trade while he waited for the time to begin his ministry.

Although descended from King David, Joseph was not royal himself. As a carpenter, he was quite a poor man, but he was kind and generous. His branch of the family had left David's city of Bethlehem in Judaea generations before, and had made their home in Nazareth, in the northern province of Galilee.

Joseph is best remembered for his loyalty to Mary in the face of an unexplained pregnancy, and his fulfilment of his fatherly duties when the real identity of his wife's son was revealed to him in dreams. This included taking flight into Egypt with Mary and the infant Jesus to escape the wrath of Herod. In 1889, Pope Leo XIII proclaimed Joseph to be the model for all fathers.

- Joseph is also patron saint of House-hunting, and of Austria, Belgium, Belize, Canada, China, Peru, Russia and South Vietnam.

CLERGY

Gabriel Possenti

Saint day: 27 February

DURING his short life of only 24 years, Gabriel Possenti spent six in the service of Christ. He was born Francis Possenti, the son of an Italian lawyer, in 1838. Although he felt the call when he was barely into his teens, Francis was having too much fun reading novels and going to see plays to answer it. Two brushes with death through illness reminded him of his destiny, but it was not until his sister died of cholera that he began studying for the priesthood, and was named Gabriel-of-our-Lady-of-Sorrows.

Then, just when his devotion seemed to promise a golden future, he was struck down by tuberculosis. The illness weakened him so much he could not perform even the most gentle priestly duties, but nevertheless he became known for his piety and was a fine example of endurance in the face of adversity. His adoption as patron for the clergy stems from the persistent call to do God's work that eventually led him to the priesthood.

COMEDIANS

Vitus

Saint day: 15 June

VITUS lived in southern Italy and was martyred in 303. He is often linked to the Fourteen Holy Helpers (saints renowned for healing who were worshipped as a group in 14th-century Germany) or to Modestus and Crescentia, supposedly his tutor and nurse.

Providing inspiration for dancers and actors, Vitus also became the patron saint for comedians because of his powers to heal sufferers of mental illness. In less enlightened times, such people were believed to be possessed of demons, and were a source of fun to those ignorant of the real reasons for their affliction. One such disorder, now known as *Sydenham's chorea*, has even retained the more generally popular name 'St Vitus' dance'.

• Vitus is also patron saint of Sicily.

DENTISTS

Apollonia

Saint day: 9 February

APOLLONIA was a deaconess in the church of Alexandria, Egypt, in the 3rd century. She was pious and virginal, and had reached her old age when she was caught up in a riot in the town, during which Christians were dragged out of their houses and murdered.

She was forced from her church and all her teeth were smashed in an attempt to make her blaspheme against God. When threatened with being burnt alive, she cheated her tormentors by actually leaping into the flames. Her martyrdom became legendary, but accounts have variously portrayed her as a young girl who had her teeth extracted by pincers, or a royal princess similarly abused by her father.

The only consistency is the loss of her teeth by brutal means, and she is portrayed in art and glass either holding a tooth in a pair of pincers or having her teeth extracted by elaborate machines of torture.

Dentists seem to have accepted the association of her pain with their profession – the quarterly magazine for Boston (USA) dentists is even called *The Apollonian*.

DOCTORS/MIDWIVES

Pantaleon

Saint day: 27 July

HAD Pantaleon remained a pagan, he would probably have become the most eminent doctor of the 4th century. Indeed, he numbered among his patients the Roman Emperor Galerius, who protected Pantaleon when he became a Christian. However, when Galerius died, Pantaleon fell foul of Emperor Diocletian and jealous colleagues denounced him during the persecutions of 303. Torture followed, and Pantaleon was eventually executed in 305.

Almost immediately, he was recognised for the saint he had been, helping the sick, often without payment. Churches were consecrated to him across the Roman Empire and, in mediaeval times, his dedication earned him a place among the Fourteen Holy Helpers.

Pantaleon was ahead of his time in all matters medical, which included childbirth, always a hazardous experience for women in those days. His adoption by midwives, too, as their patron saint is clearly an acknowledgement of his dedication to improving conditions for women in pregnancy.

• Doctors also have Luke, and Cosmas and Damian, as patron saints.

ECOLOGISTS

Francis of Assisi

Saint day: 4 October

FRANCIS of Assisi is forever linked with the love of animals, but his adoption by ecologists as their patron saint comes from his life-long habit of restoring churches which were about to fall down. Indeed, it was a voice coming from the ruins of the church of St Damian in Assisi, instructing him to build it up, that set him on the road to sainthood.

His real name was John Bernardone, the son of a cloth merchant in Assisi. He became known as Francis – the Frenchman – because his mother was French, and his father had been travelling in France on business at the time of his birth in 1181. His life was typical of that of a son of a wealthy man – fine clothes, plenty of money and a dizzy social life. He also tried his hand at soldiering in a local war, but ended up as a prisoner for a year.

After returning home and hearing the voice at St Damian's, he sold some of his father's cloth and a horse to raise money for the restoration. His father was livid and asked for the money back, while the bishop of Assisi would not accept the donation and returned it.

Undeterred, Francis renounced all his worldly goods and set about begging for money. Soon, people were moved by his example and he gathered round him a little band of followers. They lived simply in a mud hut near Assisi, and frequently went on preaching tours.

Francis' talents were many. He was a poet – his famous *Canticle of the Sun* is ever-popular – a carer of the sick, and an eloquent speaker. As his following grew, Francis also established an Order of Friars. He insisted they toe the Church line in their religious observances – Francis had no wish to set up in opposition.

Because of this, he received the help of Cardinal Uglino who eventually became Pope and who subsequently elevated Francis to sainthood only two years after his death, in 1226.

• Francis is also patron saint of Animals, and Italy.

EDITORS/JOURNALISTS/WRITERS

Francis of Sales

Saint day: 24 January

IT was Francis of Sales' conviction that the written word is more persuasive than any amount of sermons that prompted Pope Pius XI to name him patron saint of journalists in 1923, nearly 300 years after his death.

Although Francis, at 28, had only been a priest for a little over a year, he tackled the problem with a zeal that impressed his superiors. Unfortunately, however, the erring townsfolk were not at all impressed with his sermons, and he was often set upon.

His father, a wealthy nobleman from Savoy, pleaded with his son to give up such a hopeless task. But Francis was made of sterner stuff, and kept on trying to find new ways to reach the people.

He began by scribbling short leaflets and having dozens of copies made, each written by hand. He then passed them out among the townspeople. Gradually, Francis noticed that attendances at his sermons had been growing from a few hecklers to an attentive crowd and, within four years, he had succeeded in his mission.

His reward was appointment as Bishop of Geneva in 1602. Meanwhile, jottings from his missionary days were collected into one volume, aptly called *Controversies*. A second collection of writings – letters of spiritual guidance to a cousin by marriage – formed the basis of his most famous work, the *Introduction to the Devout Life*.

Francis died in 1622, and was made a saint in 1665. It was his dedication to writing, and then collecting the pieces and working them into a whole, that has inspired editors over the years.

EMBROIDERERS

Clare

Saint day: 11 August

A NATIVE of Assisi, Clare took her inspiration to live a life of poverty from St Francis of Assisi, when she was just 18, in 1212. She became a nun and founded the Order of Poor Clares in a small house next to St Damian's church in Assisi. They soon grew in number, and spread to most countries in Europe.

Clare never travelled, preferring to pray and show her devotion to God through her exquisite embroidery. Soon, every church in Assisi had an altar cloth decorated with Clare's fine needlework. Embroiderers have taken her to their hearts, mainly because she showed that stitching could convey messages and evoke emotions. She died in 1253 and was made a saint two years later.

• Clare is also patron saint of Television.

ENGINEERS

Benedict

Saint day: 11 July

B ENEDICT was the father of the monastic life, the Benedictines being the first Order of monks. Born in 480, he is thought never to have been a friar as such, but to have set up groups of devout, like-minded men so they could pray together and devote their lives to God. He lived high atop the hill of Monte Cassino in Italy, where he wrote his *Rule*, which sets out the aims of the cloistered life which have been followed by monastic orders ever since.

He has become the patron saint of engineers, not because of his devotions, but because of his ability to construct a monastery high on the jagged cliffs of Monte Cassino which has lasted nearly 1500 years.

• Benedict is patron saint of Europe, too. Engineers also have Ferdinand as patron saint.

FARMERS

Isidore

Saint day: 15 May

BORN of poor Spanish parents, early in the 12th century, Isidore became a farm labourer as soon as he was old enough to work. He was never a priest, just a poor man who lived his life as perfectly as he could. He would rise early each day and go to church, then spend the daylight hours tilling the fields. What little food he had, he shared with the poor – even the birds. Little else is known of his life, his piety coming to light only through word-of-mouth down the centuries.

Isidore has become the inspiration to farmers throughout the world because of his dedication to the soil.

FIREFIGHTERS

Laurence

Saint day: 10 August

LAURENCE perished in the persecutions of the Roman Emperor Valerian, in 258. He was a deacon of Rome and closely associated with Pope Sixtus II, who was put to the sword a few days before Laurence met his death. Laurence was buried outside the walls of Rome, and a church now stands over his tomb, appropriately called St Laurence-outside-the-wall.

Legend has it that Laurence met his end stretched and roasted on a gridiron – a martyr could hardly have been dispatched so cleanly by the sword, and therefore must have suffered a punishment somewhat more gruesome. Later writers did nothing to nail the lie, but embellished the story with grisly details, until it became acknowledged as fact.

Certainly, Laurence is depicted in art with the famous gridiron. In one marvellous mosaic in Ravenna, Italy, he carries a long cross on his shoulder and the *Gospels* in his hand as he walks through the fire to the supposed instrument of his demise. His fearlessness in the face of flames has made Laurence the guiding light for firefighters who often do the same in their daily work.

• Firefighters also have Agatha and Florian as their patron saints.

FISHERMEN

Peter

Saint day: 29 June

PETER was the first disciple called by Jesus, while he was casting his nets into the Sea of Galilee with his brother, Andrew. He is the world's best known fisherman, and it must come as no surprise that he has been adopted as patron saint of those who make their living from the sea.

His real name was Simon, but right from the very start, he was marked out as the apostle who would found the Christian Church. Jesus renamed him Peter, because the word meant 'rock' – a solid foundation for a building. Jesus saw in him a spiritual strength that, by all accounts, was not immediately apparent.

Most of what is known of Peter comes from the *New Testament*, where we meet him as a bluff, larger-than-life character given to acting hastily. He was not an educated man – ordinary people rarely were in those days – but he was sincere in his beliefs, and carried on Christ's ministry after the Ascension.

He found his way to Rome, where he fell foul of Emperor Nero, and eventually met the same fate as Christ, except that he insisted he suffer upside down, in the year 64. His remains are believed to rest in St Peter's Church in Rome.

• Fishermen also have Andrew, Simon, Zeno and Nicholas of Bari as patron saints.

FLORISTS

Rose of Lima

Saint day: 23 August

ROSE of Lima became the focus of inspiration for florists because she spent most of her short life of 31 years tending or living in her family's garden. She was born in Lima, Peru, to moderately wealthy parents in

1586. Even as a young girl, she felt drawn to God, and became convinced that the only path to perfection lay in complete self-denial. She took this to extremes, though, inflicting injury on herself. If someone commented on her beauty, she would promptly rub her face with pepper to disfigure it. Similar admiration of her hands prompted her to plunge them into lime. The burns were so horrendous that she could not dress herself for a whole month.

Her family lost what little money they had on a disastrous mining venture, and Rose helped them eke out a living by her efforts in the garden. But when they urged her to marry, she immediately took a vow of virginity and entered Holy Orders. She moved out of the house and into a hut in her beloved garden, where she lived until her final illness in 1617. Canonised in 1671, she became the first-ever saint from the New World.

• Rose of Lima is patron saint of Central America, India and Peru, too. Florists also have Dorothy and Thérèse of Lisieux as patron saints.

GLAZIERS

Lucy

Saint day: 13 December

GLAZIERS and glass-blowers have claimed Lucy as their patron saint because of her indestructible eyes. These windows on her soul were struck out by her torturers when she was imprisoned during the persecutions of the Roman Emperor Diocletian in the early 4th century. Immediately, her eyes were restored, and the miracle is celebrated, in Sweden particularly, with a Festival of Light on the shortest day of the year.

She is known to have died at Syracuse, Sicily, and the legend has sprung up that she was the daughter of a wealthy Sicilian who refused offers of marriage and gave her riches to the poor. A slighted suitor denounced her to the authorities who tortured and eventually killed her by the sword – she had escaped being burnt at the stake, again through miraculous intervention. Her body is said to lie in Venice. Most pictures and icons of Lucy, especially in mediaeval art, concentrate on her wonderful shining eyes.

- Lucy is also the patron saint of sufferers from Eye diseases.

46

GRAVE-DIGGERS AND FUNERAL DIRECTORS

Joseph of Arimathea

Saint day: 17 March

JOSEPH of Arimathea was the owner of the most famous grave in the world. He was the Jewish councillor who, as a secret follower of Jesus, asked the Romans for his body from the Cross. He then buried Jesus in a grave that had been newly hewn from the rock outside Jerusalem.

It was probably Joseph's presence at the Crucifixion which linked him, in mediaeval times, with the Holy Grail – the chalice supposed to contain Christ's blood shed on the Cross. He is said to have brought the Holy Grail to England, where he centred his preaching round Glastonbury, performing healing miracles on people from nearby towns. He is thought to be buried there, but his grave has never been found.

HAIRDRESSERS

Martin de Porres

Saint day: 3 November

MARTIN was born in Peru in 1579, the illegitimate son of a Spanish nobleman and a black maid. Although his father acknowledged him, he did not bring him up as a son of the nobility, and as a result Martin was apprenticed to a barber-surgeon by his mother when he was 12.

He joined the local Order of Dominican friars when he was 15 and turned his hand to the duties of a lay-brother at the Rosary Convent of Friars in the capital, Lima. Here, he acted as barber, gardener and tender of the sick, He paid particular attention to the slaves brought over from Africa, and also had a soft spot for all manner of small animals, including pests such as rats and mice.

He died of quatrain fever in 1639 and was made a saint nearly 200 years later, in 1837. Although also venerated for his compassion to those in need, he has been adopted, too, as patron of those who ply the trade he learned as a boy.

• Martin is also patron saint of Social justice.

HEALTH INSPECTORS

Raphael

Saint day: 29 September

RAPHAEL is one of three archangels referred to in the Bible. He is mentioned most often in the apocryphal *Book of Tobit*, and is reputed to be the angel who moved the waters of the healing pool in Jerusalem. People afflicted with all manner of diseases somehow got to the pool and climbed into it. Many were known to have been restored to health due to immersion in its waters.

Health inspectors have adopted him as their mentor because of this association with healing. He is usually depicted in art with the other archangels, Michael and Gabriel, and is distinguished by the presence of his companion, Tobit, and a fish.

HOTELIERS/PUBLICANS

Gentian

Saint day: 11 December

GENTIAN was an obscure pagan Gaul, who lived at Sains, France, in the early 9th century, and who had fame thrust upon him because he was kind-hearted to the beleaguered Christian missionaries, Fuscian and Victoricus.

These two had been sent from Rome to convert the Gauls and team up with St Quentin, who had established himself at Amiens. When they got there, they found that the town was in uproar, and that anti-Christian feeling was running high. They retreated to Sains, where Gentian offered them hospitality until the furore died down.

Unfortunately, Fuscian and Victoricus were denounced to the pagan governor, Rictovarius, who promptly besieged Gentian's house with a posse of soldiers. Gentian met them at the door with his sword drawn. Although not a Christian himself, he could not abide intolerance, and was ready to die for the freedom to worship. Accordingly, Rictovarius had him beheaded on the spot, and took away his guests in irons. They were later executed.

For his unconditional kindness in taking in the missionaries, Gentian the pagan has become the patron saint of hoteliers and inn-keepers.

HOUSEWIVES/COOKS

Martha

Saint day: 29 July

MARTHA has symbolised the thankless task of keeping hearth and home together ever since Jesus is said to have chided her gently for complaining that her sister, Mary, never shared in the preparations when he came to visit, but sat at his feet, listening to him preaching. She is often portrayed with the instruments of her calling – a ladle, a broom, and a bunch of keys.

• Martha is also invoked as the patron saint of Lay sisters in a convent community, representing the active life, rather than a contemplative one.

JEWELLERS/GOLDSMITHS/ AND BLACKSMITHS

Eloi

Saint day: 1 December

ELOI was a goldsmith by trade, practising his art in early 7th-century France. He became known for his economic use of raw materials as well as for his artistry, and was commissioned by successive kings to create chalices, crosses and plaques for early Christian churches. The last of his known pieces of gold working, a chalice kept at Chelles, disappeared during the French Revolution.

He took Holy Orders, and eventually rose to become Bishop of Noyon in 641. Christianity had only recently come to France, and Eloi made it his business to rail against pagan practices, such as fortune-telling. He is now patron saint of those working with precious metals, stones and iron.

JUDGES

Ivo of Kermartin

Saint day: 19 May

IVO Hélory was born in the small town of Tréguier, near Kermartin in Brittany, in 1253. His father was Lord of the Manor there, and could well afford to send Ivo to school in Paris when the boy was 14. He spent 10 years studying philosophy, theology and canon law, and then went on to master civil law at Orléans. Whilst a student, Ivo did not indulge in the excesses of his peers, but led a monk-like existence, even down to a hair shirt, a bread-and-water diet, and a straw mat for a bed.

On returning to Brittany, Ivo was appointed to judge cases in the ecclesiastical courts at Rennes. He was very impartial and just, especially concerning the plight of orphans and the poor in general. He eventually returned to his home town in the same capacity.

Meanwhile, Ivo had become more and more devout. In 1284, he was ordained priest and assigned the parish of Trédrez. Before long, he felt he had to choose between his callings, and gave up his judicial post in 1287 to spend the rest of his life ministering to the disadvantaged. By now, he had made a name for himself for persuading his petitioners to settle out of court rather than face the heavy expense of a trial – clearly, a man who would recognise the burdens of litigation in the modern world.

LAUNDRY WORKERS

Veronica

Saint day: 12 July

V ERONICA is a mysterious woman, known only for her place in legend, which tells us that she lived in Jerusalem at the time of the Roman occupation, where it was usual for the people to crowd the streets to watch wrongdoers and enemies of the state forced-marched to a gruesome death by crucifixion on Calvary hill outside the city.

Veronica was no exception. One day, on leaving her household duties, cloth still in hand, to witness the passing of the latest batch of prisoners, she was over-come with compassion at the sight of someone who seemed to have been treated so badly that he could hardly walk, much less stagger under the weight of his cross. As he collapsed, Veronica rushed forward to wipe his face, before surly Roman guards threw her back into the crowd. When she examined her cloth, she was astounded to find his face imprinted on it: the wretch on whom she had taken pity was none other than Jesus Christ, and the imprint came to be seen to be nothing short of a miracle.

Seven centuries passed before a cloth bearing Christ's features surfaced in Rome, where it was lodged in the Church of St Peter, under the title 'Veronica's veil'. Immediately, it became an object of devotion, which continued well into the 20th century.

Speculations as to Veronica's identity range from a sister of Martha and Mary, in whose house Jesus often dined, and whose brother, Lazarus, he raised from the dead, to the wife of tax collector, Zaccheus, who hid in a tree to watch Jesus pass by, during his preaching years. A favourite, however, is the woman who had been healed by Christ from internal bleeding, and who came forward to pay her debt to him.

Although no historical proof exists that she was any of these people, the concept of a woman so moved to pity that she risked her own safety to minister to the stricken Christ has captured the imagination of Christians down the ages. It is her act of washing the Saviour's face which has made her patron saint of laundry workers.

LAWYERS

Hilary

Saint day: 13 January

HILARY was born in Poitiers, France, of a wealthy family. He married, had one daughter and lived a pagan life until his conversion to Christianity in 350, at the age of about 35. So devout was he that he set about correcting misconceptions about Christianity which were rife at the time.

He wrote tracts and defended his case at numerous councils and synods. At one time, his refusal to bow to current thinking earned him three years in exile. On his return, he persuaded the people of Poitiers, by dint of reason and argument, to return to orthodox Christian beliefs. He died there in 368.

Hilary's persistence in debate won him adoption as patron saint for lawyers. His name is also lent to the second term in the academic year – the Hilary Term – at the Law Courts and at some universities, which begins on his Feast Day.

• Lawyers also have Sir Thomas More as patron saint.

LIBRARIANS

Jerome

Saint day: 30 September

JEROME'S greatest achievement was the organisation of the texts of the books of the Bible and their translation into Latin from the original. He was born in northern Italy in 342 and received a good education, especially in classical languages and literature. He travelled widely until, in 366, he decided that he had the calling to become a monk.

He settled in the town of Aquileia, a centre for religious learning. But, being a hot-tempered man, prone to causing arguments, he left there amid controversy in 374, travelling to Antioch in the Holy Land, where he was ordained, and then to the desert in Syria. He remained there for five years, learning Hebrew and studying the Scriptures.

After his life as a hermit, Jerome rejoined civilisation, first travelling to Constantinople, then Rome. In both cities, he embarked on translations of the Scriptures into a Latin 'Vulgate' version of the Bible. He stayed in Rome only three years, having to leave, in 385, because he had upset so many people with his quick temper.

He settled finally in Bethlehem, where he established an order of monks and spent the rest of his life teaching, studying and writing. Jerome's dedication to the organisation of the Bible and insistence on accuracy makes him the ideal role-model for librarians.

LIGHTHOUSEKEEPERS

Clement

Saint day: 23 November

CLEMENT was the fourth Pope of the Christian Church who made it his business to organise its administration, most notably in Corinth as well as Rome. His zeal, however, irritated the Roman hierarchy, and he was exiled to the Crimea. Although made to work in the mines there, he carried on preaching and soon had enough converts to open 75 churches.

Whether this was too much for the still-pagan authorities, no historical records exist to say, but Clement was killed for his pains in about the year 100 by being thrown into the sea with an anchor tied around his neck. It is said his tomb on the sea bed, created by angels, is visible once a year at exceptionally low tides. Seven hundred years later, missionaries found what they thought were Clement's bones and took them to Rome where they lie buried in the church of San Clemente.

In paintings, Clement is usually depicted with an anchor, the instrument of his martyrdom, and is patron of the Guild of the Undivided Trinity of London (Trinity House), the body responsible for lighthouses and lightships.

• Lighthousekeepers also have Dunstan and Venerius as patron saints.

MAGISTRATES

Ferdinand III of Castile

Saint day: 30 May

FERDINAND became King of the Spanish provinces of Castile, in 1217, and Leon, in 1230. He was a warrior king as well as a devout Christian, and saw it as his mission in life to retrieve Spanish lands which had been occupied by the Moslem Moors, bringing back most of Andalusia to Christianity. He did not persecute the Moslems, but sent Franciscan friars to convert them.

In an age when might was right, Ferdinand became well-known for his administration of impartial justice, making him the ideal saint for magistrates who strive to do the same in modern times.

Miners/Gunners

Barbara

Saint day: 4 December

Details of Barbara's life are sketchy – some say because she did not exist at all – but it appears she was martyred in the persecutions of the Roman Emperor Diocletian, in about the year 303. Legend has it that her father shut her up in a tower so no man should see her. However, while he was away, although there was a queue of suitors for her hand in marriage, Barbara decided to become a Christian instead, and began the life of a hermit in a bath house in her father's garden.

Upon his return, her father was so incensed at her conversion to Christianity that he handed her over to judges who sentenced her to death. By strange coincidence, her father was killed by lightning, almost at the hour of her martyrdom. This was the basis of her adoption as patron by those in danger of sudden death, such as miners and also gunners.

MISSIONARIES

Francis Xavier

Saint day: 3 December

BORN in 1506 to a Spanish nobleman from Xavier, near Navarre in northern Spain, Francis left home at the age of 18 to attend the University of Paris. There he became firm friends with fellow Spaniard Ignatius Loyola, who was to found the Society of Jesus in 1537, the year the two men were ordained as priests in Venice.

The aim of the Society was to spread the Christian faith abroad and so, in 1541, Francis set sail for India, landing on the island of Goa, off Bombay, 13 months later. He started with shaking up the lapsed Catholics on Goa and, encouraged by his success, branched out to convert the native population. He won them over by simplifying complicated precepts and setting them to the music of the popular songs of the day.

Over the next seven years, Francis made his way across India, and travelled as far as present-day Malaysia. In 1549, he set sail for Japan, where he made converts, but in much smaller numbers – only 100 in his first 12 months. It was evident that he needed the support of the ruling Mikado, so he mustered enough respectable clothes and appropriate gifts to present himself at the Japanese Court, where he was accepted. Through this, he was able to make 2000 converts although, in the years after his departure, these suffered merciless persecution.

After returning briefly to Goa, Francis set out on the mission he had dreamed about for years – China. He never made it to the shore, however. Suffering severely from sea-sickness and fever, he was dumped on the beach at San-Chian Island, at the mouth of the River Canton. He lay there for some days, until a friendly Portuguese merchant took pity on him and gave him shelter. But the damage was done, and Francis died in the early hours of 3 December 1552, with only a Chinese convert called Antony, a Portuguese man and two slaves by his side. He was just 46 years old.

Francis' body was packed in quicklime and taken to Goa, where its burial site soon became a place of pilgrimage. His right arm found its way to Rome in 1615, where it reposes in the Church of Gésu. Francis was canonized in 1622, and named patron of Roman Catholic overseas missions by Pope Pius XI in 1927.

• Francis Xavier is also patron saint of Borneo, India, Japan, Outer Mongolia and Pakistan.

MOUNTAINEERS

Bernard of Aosta

Saint day: 28 May

ALSO known as Bernard of Menthon, and born in 996 of Italian parents, the patron saint of mountaineers was first a priest, and then vicar-general of Aosta, high in the Italian Alps. As well as founding schools and churches, Bernard took special care of mountain travellers, building guest houses in which they could take shelter from extreme weather.

It was also he who instigated the system of mountain rescue for travellers lost in snow drifts, using specially trained large dogs, the breed now called St Bernard.

Although Bernard died in 1081, it was not until over 800 years later, in 1923, that he was named patron saint of mountaineers by Pope Pius XI, himself a keen mountaineer.

• Bernard is also patron saint of Skiers.

MUSICIANS

Cecilia

Saint day: 22 November

C ECILIA has been patroness of musicians since the 16th century, when the Academy of Music in Rome was founded in 1584. The association arose from legendary writings about her, describing an organ playing at her wedding when she vowed to remain constant to God and to preserve her virginity

The legend goes on to say that her husband accepted her decision and converted to Christianity himself, but was martyred soon afterwards. Cecilia, in turn, was persecuted, but attempts to execute her by suffocation failed, as did beheading. Three blows failed to kill her right away, but she died of the wounds three days later.

English poets have perpetuated her links with music, notably Chaucer in *The Canterbury Tales*, then the 17th-century poets John Dryden, in his *Song for St Cecilia's Day*, and Alexander Pope, in the work *Ode for Music on St Cecilia's Day*.

Early representations of Cecilia show no musical instruments – testament to her late adoption; but post-16th-century depictions often include an organ or some other musical instrument, such as a lute.

• Cecilia is also patron saint of Singers.

NURSES

Camillus

Saint day: 14 July

CAMILLUS came to God the hard way. A bluff giant of a soldier, given to bad temper, he gambled away all his money in 1574, when he was just 24 years old. Even his shirt was stripped from his back in a Naples street to pay gambling debts. On top of this, Camillus had contracted an ulcer in one of his legs in the Turkish wars which made the limb unsightly and painful. Life was not easy for Camillus.

In such a pitiful state, Camillus turned to God, but could not join the Franciscan friars as he wanted to, because of his medical problem. The friars existed to travel and spread the Word – a man with a bad leg was not much use to them.

Instead, Camillus dedicated himself to caring for the sick. He was appalled at the way they were treated by indifferent and surly servants, so he formed a body of men specifically to nurse them back to health. He founded hospitals, visited the sick in their homes and, in 1595 and 1601, sent bands of nurses to the battlefields of Hungary and Croatia.

Even though his own body was riddled with disease in later life – a rupture, foot sores, bowel trouble – Camillus struggled on. He died, aged 64, in Genoa, and was made a saint in 1746. Nearly 200 years later, he was named patron of nurses because of his supreme example of selflessness and compassion.

• Nurses also have Elizabeth of Hungary and John of God as patron saints.

PAWNBROKERS

Nicholas of Bari

Saint day: 6 December

ST Nicholas is known the world over as the enchanted being, Santa Claus, who descends into children's homes at Christmas time to leave them presents. But little is known of his actual life.

Records show that he was Bishop of Myra, in Turkey, in the early 4th century, and that his bones were removed from there to Bari in Italy, after an unseemly competition with Rome who also wanted the relics, in 1087.

His association with pawnbrokers comes from a story in which he saved three sisters from prostitution by giving their father three bags of gold so they could marry with a dowry. (Three balls have now come to symbolise the pawnbrokers' trade). There is, however, no evidence that Nicholas ever took pledges.

• Nicholas is also patron saint of Brides, Children, Business people, Fishermen, Unmarried women, Pilgrims, and of Russia.

PHILATELISTS/ AND POST OFFICE WORKERS

Gabriel

Saint day: 29 September

The Archangel Gabriel has been adopted as the patron saint of telecommunications, including the Post Office, and also stamp collectors. This association arose because of his Biblical role as bringer of news – principally, the birth of John the Baptist and the announcement to Mary she was to be the mother of Jesus. Other visitations by an angel – appearing to the shepherds in the fields outside Bethlehem and to Joseph in a dream warning of Herod's plot to kill Jesus – may also have been Gabriel.

POLICE OFFICERS

Michael

Saint day: 29 September

OF the three Archangels mentioned in the Bible, Michael is regarded as the most powerful. He fights with the Devil on two recorded occasions in the *New Testament* – once, verbally, over the body of Moses in the *Epistle of Jude*, and physically, in the *Book of Revelation*, for the control of the Heavens. This book also records that Michael's power is such that he can weigh souls at the Last Judgement.

A reference in the *Old Testament* describes him as the guardian of Israel, while later writings, such as the 2nd-century *Shepherd of Hermas*, give him a firmer say in the lives of the people: 'He governs them, for it was he who gave them the Law.'

What better personage for the police to take as their example than one of God's most trusted aides?

• Michael is also patron saint of Germany and Papua New Guinea.

SAILORS

Francis of Paola

Saint day: 2 April

FRANCIS of Paola's association with the sea dates from very early in his life. As a young friar, he went on pilgrimages to Assisi and Rome. After returning, he settled in a cave overlooking the sea near Paola. Isolation was shortlived, however. Two companions came to join him when he was 20. When more followed, he gave up the idea of a solitary life and founded an Order of friars who were to be known as 'Minims' for the harsh life they led.

Even while he was alive, he performed miracles, most of which were connected with the sea, and so he has come to be adopted as protector of seafarers. Later in life, he travelled to France, to attend the deathbed of King Louis XI, where he died in 1507. He was made a saint in 1519.

• Sailors also have Phocas, Brendan and Erasmus as patron saints.

SCHOLARS

Thomas Aquinas

Saint day: 28 January

IT is hardly surprising that the saint most noted for his excellent education and years of study and writing should become the patron saint of scholars. But it almost did not happen that way. As the son of a wealthy Italian family, Thomas Aquinas automatically received the best education money could buy. In 13th-century Italy, that meant the Benedictine monastery at Monte Cassino, which Thomas attended from the age of five to 13, followed by five years at Naples University.

A glittering future awaited him – his parents were confident he could become Abbot of Monte Cassino. But they were horrified when he decided the life of a poor friar was for him. To add insult to injury, he chose the Dominican friars, an Order who existed on alms – beggars to the lay people.

In desperation, Thomas' father had him imprisoned at their home for over a year to rid his head of this nonsense, but to no avail. Thomas entered the Dominican Order in 1244, and spent 30 years teaching and studying.

His work-rate was phenomenal – it is said that he could dictate to four secretaries at a time, on different subjects. His writings on the Christian faith are required reading by theologians even today.

• Scholars also have Bede and Jerome as patron saints.

SCIENTISTS

Albert the Great

Saint day: 15 November

BORN in 1206 to a noble family from Swabia, now part of Switzerland, Albert decided early on that he was going to enter Holy Orders. He chose the Dominican friars and joined their house in Padua, Italy. He was principally a teacher, but by dint of hard work, scaled the hierarchy of the mediaeval church to become bishop of Ratisbon in 1260.

Alas, he was no good at organising – an essential part of the job at that time – so he gave up the post after only two years and went back to his books.

His abiding passion, after theology, was science, and the last 18 years of his life were devoted to scientific study. Among his famous works are treatises on astronomy and chemistry, all the more remarkable because Europe had only just emerged from the Dark Ages and such refined subjects were still regarded as sorcery. Albert's tenacity in his studies makes him a shining example for scientists as they persevere to advance human knowledge.

SECRETARIES

Cassian of Imola

Saint day: 13 August

CASSIAN'S origins are shrouded in the mists of time, but it is certain that he was martyred at the height of the Roman persecutions. This places him in the early centuries after Christianity spread across the known world. He was a schoolmaster from Imola, 27 miles outside Ravenna, northern Italy, and also a Christian. On discovery, he was brought before the local governor, who handed him over to a particularly nasty judge to pass sentence.

Cassian was taken out amidst 200 boys whom he had taught in the past – and who, inevitably, had old scores to settle – and left to their mercy. There was none, of course. Instead, this juvenile mob proceeded to stab him with their iron pens (sharpened at one end for writing on wax tablets), some fiendishly carving letters into his flesh. The pain must have been excruciating.

Cassian died from his wounds and was buried locally, at Imola. His fame, however, reached Rome, where early depictions in art show him dying amid a thousand stab wounds. It is his connection with writing, and its instruments, which has led to his association with modern scribes and secretaries.

SHOEMAKERS

Crispin and Crispinian

Saint day: 25 October

THESE two 3rd-century Romans were cobblers by trade, and they made their living by it to avoid relying on hand-outs while preaching in Gaul (France). Although martyred there in 285, legend has it that they came to England and settled in Faversham, Kent, setting up business in a house in Preston Street now occupied by the Swan Inn. Pilgrims visited the house as late as the 17th century, and an altar in their honour stands in Faversham parish church.

England won the battle of Agincourt, during the Hundred Years' War with France, on their Feast Day in 1415, and Shakespeare acknowledged the English connection with the Roman saints in his play, *Henry V.*

• The patronage of Crispin and Crispinian also extends from Shoe-makers to Leather-workers in general.

SOCIAL WORKERS

Louise de Marillac

Saint day: 15 March

LOUISE was born to a wealthy French aristocrat in 1591. Her mother died when she was a small child, but her father sent her to nuns at Poissy to be educated and also taught her himself. He, too, died when she was only 15. Louise harboured ideas of entering a nunnery, but instead married Antony Le Gras, by whom she had a son, Michael, and with whom she enjoyed 12 years of happily married life until his untimely death in 1625.

Vowing never to marry again, Louise returned to her girlhood wish to serve. She had no idea how until she met Vincent de Paul, later saint, a well-known cleric who founded institutions to help the poor. At this time, he was organising wealthy Christian ladies to help minister to the needy and, eventually convinced of Louise's sincerity, allowed her to join.

It very soon became clear that the refined ladies could not cope with the appalling conditions which confronted them in the slums, and Vincent instead recruited devout, poorer-class women to do the dirty work while the ladies were put to raising funds.

Louise, however, was made of sterner stuff, and Vincent allowed her to carry on. Moreover, he charged her with the training of young peasant girls and widows for work amongst the poor and sick. She took four of them into her house in the unfashionable district of rue des Fosses-St Victor, and from these beginnings began the Sisters of Charity.

But Vincent was not convinced they would be effective as a religious Order, and so they remained lay-sisters who took vows only yearly. Soon, though, hospitals were passing on their cases to the Sisters of Charity, to minister to them once their medical needs had been attended to, and the Charity also took on the responsibility of teaching and caring for abandoned children.

Louise's health finally broke from the rigours of her selfless life, and she died after a long illness in 1660. She was canonised in 1934, and has become the patron saint of social workers for her early lead in recognising that the poor, sick and neglected need support in order to enable them to lead satisfactory lives.

• Social workers also have John Francis Regis as patron saint.

SOLDIERS

George

Saint day: 23 April

GEORGE has been the patron saint of soldiers for nearly a thousand years. He was a soldier himself, and was martyred for his faith during the persecutions carried out by the Roman Emperor Diocletian, in the early 4th century. But it is for the legend of his remarkably brave confrontation with a dragon that he is perhaps best known.

We are told that he came across a town in Asia Minor which was being terrorised by a dragon that lived in a swamp on the outskirts. Attempts to kill it were repulsed by its fiery breath, and the beast exacted a ransom of two sheep per day from the terrified townsfolk.

When sheep grew scarce, human sacrifices were chosen by lot, one of which fell to the ruler's daughter. She dressed herself as a bride and rode out to her doom, whereupon George appeared and attacked the dragon with his lance. He borrowed the maiden's girdle and led the captive beast into the town, promising to slay the dragon if the people turned to Jesus Christ. In the circumstances, they all flocked to be baptised – 15,000 men are said to have converted on the spot – and George was as good as his word.

His fame through this legend spread rapidly, and it was written down so many times that it gradually began to have a ring of truth about it. Over the centuries, soldiers have looked to him as the perfect example of bravery in battle, and he became their patron saint. Indeed, George was called upon to lend his weight to the Crusaders' side in their war against the Saracens in the 13th century. And after a vision of George appeared to his armies at the siege of Antioch, Richard the Lionheart declared him the patron saint of England.

• Soldiers also have Maurice as their patron saint.

SURGEONS

Cosmas and Damian

Saint day: 26 September

COSMAS and Damian were, reputedly, twin brothers who became doctors and administered their skills without charge. Their association with surgery has indeed been depicted in several works of art. The most spectacular is a 15th-century example, now in the Society of Antiquaries, London, which shows Cosmas and Damian grafting a new, white leg on to the live body of a black man.

When they lived is not known, but churches in their name date from the 5th century. A basilica built at Cyrrhus in Turkey commemorates their martyrdom there. The 15th-century wealthy Medici family promoted the cult of Cosmas and Damian in Italy – unexpected in view of the Medicis' obsession with making money, whereas the saints seem to have had no interest at all in this pursuit.

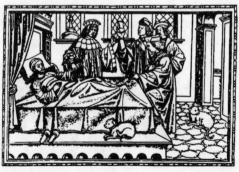

TAXI DRIVERS

Fiacre

Saint day: 1 September

IT seems ironic that a hermit should be chosen as patron saint for a trade so closely associated with people, but Fiacre became patron saint of taxi drivers in a rather roundabout way.

He was an Irishman who settled in France in the mid-7th century. His devotion and insistence on the solitary life, or 'exile for Christ', as he put it, led to his sainthood in the early Middle Ages. But while his native Ireland has always been lukewarm about him, his adopted country put up shrines to Fiacre, and his popularity reached its height there in the 17th and 18th centuries.

Not only were churches named after him, but also buildings, one of which was the sumptuous Hôtel Saint-Fiacre in Paris. It was from here that horse-drawn cabs plied their trade in the 19th century. So close was their association with the hotel that the word *fiacre* even entered the French language as the word for taxi-cab.

TEACHERS

John Baptist de la Salle

Saint day: 7 April

JOHN decided he wanted to be a priest very early in life, beginning the long road to ordination when he was just eleven, in 1662, and entering the priesthood in 1678, at the age of twenty seven. He came from a noble family in Reims, France, and used his money to open schools for poor boys who, otherwise, would have had no education.

At first, he rented a building, but soon moved his pupils into his own house. Almost immediately, two of his brothers moved out, as did several schoolmasters. However, John managed to engage more and from then on dedicated his whole life to education. He gave up his position as a canon of Reims and sold all his goods, using the proceeds for a famine-relief campaign in the Champagne region.

Four more schools were opened, and John persuaded the new teachers to band together to form a religious brotherhood, increasing their numbers with his own school-leavers. Word went round that his education methods were extremely effective and, very soon, local priests were sending him prospective teachers for training, so that they could bring back his ideas to their village schools.

John saw that his modest school was hopelessly inadequate for the resultant rush of trainees, and he founded

the first college for teacher-training in Reims, in 1686.
More colleges were opened in France, and then England.

No-one had ever seen a régime like it. He abandoned
Latin as a medium for instruction, and taught his pupils
in their own language. He also insisted on silence in the
classroom, forbidding the usual free-for-all that blighted
other seats of learning. Indeed, his strict discipline led to
the opening of schools for delinquents – the forerunners
of the 'Approved School' system that existed in later
centuries.

By the time John died, in 1719 at the age of 68, the
Order he had established, now called the Brothers of
Christian Schools, had become the most vigorous force
in the education of poor Catholic boys. Today, there are
20,000 members worldwide. John was canonised in
1900, and became patron saint of teachers in 1950.

DAILY LIFE

ARE you a regular air passenger but scared of flying? Are you taking an examination but not sure if you'll pass? Are you going on a skiing holiday, but frightened of falling and breaking your leg? Saints with even the most slender associations have been adopted to assist in situations like these. In fact, many problems we encounter during the course of our everyday lives are associated with a patron saint who may be invoked to help. Even inanimate objects can have patron saints – motorways, for example, have John the Baptist, who announced he had been sent to 'make straight the ways of the Lord'. As you read on, you will find that the most ordinary activities and everyday dangers to which we are exposed have a saint who is designated to help us through.

ACCUSED (FALSELY)

Raymund Nonnatus

Saint day: 31 August

RAYMOND acquired his curious name at the hour of his birth, in Catalonia, Spain, in about the year 1204. Translated from the Latin *Non natus*, it means 'not born' and refers to his coming into the world after his mother had died during the rigours of labour.

He was a good Christian, as a child, and his doting father consented to him entering the Order of Mercedarians in Barcelona where, in due course, he became a monk. Raymond was assigned the formidable task of converting the 'Infidel' – Moslems. He set sail for North Africa, and spent many fruitful years among the slaves in Algiers, bringing a large number to Christ.

When his money ran out, however, he was thrown into prison and there followed eight months of incarceration during which he faced a series of trials on trumped-up charges. Eventually, his Order paid a ransom for him, and he returned to Spain in 1239.

Although only 35, his health was broken by the ordeal. As a result, when he was nominated as a Cardinal by Pope Gregory IX, the journey to Rome proved too much for him and he died on the way, in 1240.

• Raymund Nonnatus is also patron saint of Midwives, as a tribute to the dedication of their mediaeval predecessors who saved his life at birth.

ANIMALS

Francis of Assisi

Saint day: 4 October

FRANCIS was born John Bernardone in 1181, in the Italian town of Assisi, where he was nick-named Francis – the Frenchman – because of his French mother. He was not immediately marked out for sainthood. His family was wealthy and, as a young man, he enjoyed all the trappings which that life provided. He even ventured his luck as a soldier, but was captured and spent a year in prison.

Undeterred, Francis bought expensive armour and set off to fight in another war but, on the way, he met a poor man whose clothes scarcely covered his back. Something compelled Francis to swap garments, and he continued his journey in the rags of the poor man – who was probably somewhat bewildered at having a suit of armour thrust upon him.

Francis had not progressed very far when he heard a voice telling him to turn back, which he did. Gradually, he felt drawn to help others, and began to spend much of his time ministering to the sick in the local hospital. While praying in the church of St Damian, a voice said he should repair its fabric. Francis then resolved to give away all he had and lead a life of poverty and devotion. The money was used to restore this and other Assisi churches, while Francis lived in a little cottage outside the town gates, with others who had been drawn to his example.

Thereafter, Francis spent his time wandering wherever he thought God's word needed to be preached – he even ventured to Africa to convert the Moslems. As time went on, his Order grew, until it was some 5,000 strong at the time of his death in 1226. Francis was canonised by Pope Gregory IX and his Order spread all over Europe. He is remembered for his piety and love of all God's creatures, which included all birds and animals with which he was known to have a remarkable affinity. Because of this, he has become their patron saint.

• Francis is also patron saint of Ecologists, and of Italy.

BABIES

The Holy Innocents

Saint day: 28 December

The Holy Innocents were those baby boys under two years old who were slaughtered in Bethlehem on the orders of King Herod, who had heard from the Magi of the birth of Jesus, whom they called King. Herod hoped to eliminate any opposition by killing Jesus but, as he did not know who Jesus was nor when, precisely, he had been born, he ordered his soldiers to kill all the baby boys. These babies have always held a special place in the Christian Church because they died in place of Jesus.

They are the patron saints of all babies, but they are particularly invoked to console the parents of children dying in infancy.

BRIDES

Nicholas of Bari

Saint day: 6 December

As bishop of Myra, in 4th-century Turkey, Nicholas was in a position to help all those who came to his churches for the sacraments. One of these was marriage, and many times he must have advised prospective brides of their forthcoming duties to God, and their husbands, on marriage. But it is probably the legend of his saving three girls from prostitution by providing them with dowries that established him as the helper of young women who wish to secure for themselves a prosperous and happy union. This same story led to his becoming patron saint of pawnbrokers, the three dowries now being represented by the three-balls sign.

• Nicholas is also the patron saint of Children, Pilgrims, Pawnbrokers, Unmarried women, Sailors, Business people, Fishermen and of Russia.

Children

Nicholas of Bari

Saint day: 6 December

NICHOLAS established a reputation as a 'wonder-worker', many miracles having been attributed to his intercession with God. He became venerated locally very soon after his death, but it was through the transfer of his relics from Myra to Bari, in Italy, that his fame became widespread in western Europe.

His first association with children comes from a very early episode in his life when, as a baby, he refused his mother's breast on Wednesdays and Fridays. The reason for this is unknown, but is possibly an extreme interpretation of a religious observance. And in later life, Nicholas is said to have brought back to life three boys who had been drowned in a vat of brine by a butcher.

This reputation for caring for children has developed, in western Christianity, into a cult of St Nicholas, more popularly known as 'Santa Claus', Legend has it that he appears at Christmas, silently creeping into houses at dead of night, to leave presents for children. In many countries, he comes on Christmas Eve but, in Holland and Germany, presents are delivered late on his Feast Day. Otherwise, he is invoked to intercede on behalf of children, if they are ill or in need of guidance.

• Nicholas is also the patron saint of Brides, Pilgrims, Pawnbrokers, Unmarried women, Sailors, Business people, Fishermen and of Russia.

CHILDREN (ILLEGITIMATE)

John Francis Regis

Saint day: 16 June

JOHN was born in 1597, the son of French landed gentry. At that time, well-to-do Catholic families sent their sons to be educated by Jesuits to stiffen their faith in the face of Protestantism, and so it was with John. He attended a college near the family home, in the Narbonne district of northern France, and was so taken with the dedication of the Order that he joined as soon as he was 18, in 1615.

John proved a good novice, and was often to be found teaching poor children. He was ordained, after long years of study, and was then groomed for missionary work and sent to Languedoc, in the south of France, to bring lapsed Catholics back to the faith.

He was no great orator, and the crowds gathered to make fun of him, but the simplicity of his message soon had them asking forgiveness. He appealed to all social classes, but preferred to concentrate his talents on helping the poor. He made it his business to visit the meanest homes, the filthiest prisons, and the most pestilential hospitals, to offer guidance and hope to the wretched inmates.

He was particularly concerned with women who had turned to prostitution for a living, often to support illegitimate children. He found great satisfaction in redeeming them from their low life, by providing refuges.

It is his work with these women, and with other poor women abandoned with children, that led to John Francis Regis becoming the patron saint of illegitimate children. It is a patronage still existing today, in spite of the fact that in most parts of the world there is now little stigma to giving birth out of wedlock.

John spent the rest of his life in south-east France, patiently bringing back to the faith whole regions where lawlessness and immorality had taken over. He was only 43 when, worn out by his ceaseless work and austere life, he contracted pleurisy after being caught in bad weather on his way to a new mission at La Louvrec. He managed to struggle there and preach on Christmas Day, but died one week later, on 31 December 1640. He is buried at La Louvrec, and his shrine is still regularly visited by pilgrims.

CROPS

Magnus of Fussen

Saint day: 6 September

MAGNUS was born in 696, but nothing is known of his early life. He became a monk at the monastery of St Gall, France, but he also undertook missionary work, in Switzerland and Germany. In about the year 750, Magnus was sent to Fussen to establish a monastery of the Benedictine Order. He spent the next 22 years in missionary work, and was still working to bring souls to Christ when he died in 772, aged 76.

He was very popular in Switzerland, and the story went round that he used to bless fields there with a staff given to him by St Columba, whereupon all the vermin hiding among the crops, and systematically munching their way through them, fled, never to return. He gained a reputation, at least in legend, for being able to protect crops in this way. Now, as patron saint for the protection of crops, Magnus is invoked against all elements which can cause damage, including storms.

DISASTERS

Genevieve

Saint day: 3 January

GENEVIEVE was born in Nanterre, France, some time in the middle of the 5th century – her exact year of birth is not known – and began her novitiate for the cloistered life when she was only 15. When her parents died, Genevieve moved to Paris, where she continued her retiring, contemplative existence.

She stepped in to help her adopted city on two occasions – when it was threatened with starvation through siege by the Frankish king, Childeric, and when attacked by Attila the Hun. To avert the first, she boldly led out bands of armed men to bring back food. To ward off the second, she instructed the frightened Parisians to fast and pray. Both potential disasters were avoided and she has always been called upon subsequently by people facing extreme circumstances, and especially the French in times of national crisis.

Genevieve died in about the year 500, and her remains were laid to rest at the church of St Peter and St Paul, later called St Genevieve's, in Paris, which became a shrine for pilgrims. This was largely destroyed during the French Revolution, and on its site now stands a burial place for civic dignitaries, known as the Panthéon.

• Genevieve is also the patron saint of Fever sufferers.

EARTHQUAKES

Emygdius

Saint day: 9 August

NOT much is known of the life and times of Emygdius, only that he was beheaded in the course of the persecutions of the Roman Emperor Diocletian in 304, but legend has it that he came from the town of Trier in Germany, converted to Christianity and subsequently went to Rome.

Almost as soon as Emygdius got there, he happened to go into a heathen temple and, enraged by the graven images he found, brought one crashing to the ground. Needless to say, the Roman authorities took great exception to this deliberate affront, and he was only saved from dire punishment by swift ordination as a bishop by the then Pope.

Emygdius was now sent out into the surrounding countryside to convert, which he did with some success until Diocletian caught up with him.

He has been adopted as the patron saint of earthquakes, probably from the effects of bringing crashing down to earth that gigantic stone statue, and is particularly favoured by the United States cities of San Francisco and Los Angeles, constantly at risk from earthquake damage.

Examinations

Joseph of Cupertino

Saint day: 18 September

JOSEPH was born in Cupertino, near the town of Brindisi in southern Italy. He entered the priesthood in 1628, at the age of 25, having passed the required examinations. This was remarkable because he had no education to speak of when young, being the son of a carpenter so inept that he had to sell his house to pay debts and lived thereafter in the garden shed.

When opportunities did present themselves – service in an order of Capuchin friars – Joseph failed even in the most humble duties of a kitchen hand by dropping the plates and letting the fire go out. But, strangely, he was good at examinations, and he has been taken on, therefore, as the beacon for examination candidates, probably on the basis that if he could do it, anyone can. He is known, too, for his extraordinary ability to levitate himself at will.

• Joseph is also patron saint of Air crews, Air passengers, Astronauts and Flying in general.

HARVESTS

Antony of Padua

Saint day: 13 June

A s far as is known, Antony never, himself, went out into the fields to sow and reap, yet he has been chosen to represent those who would pray for a successful harvest. This is because, as a preacher, his harvest was one of souls.

Born in 1195 to a noble Portuguese family from Lisbon, Ferdinand – he took the name Antony later – decided on a life of devotion early, and spent his late teens and early twenties working his way up to become a full Franciscan friar in 1220.

Soon after, he was sent to Morocco to try to convert those who had lately put to death several colleagues. Illness struck him down almost as soon as he got there, and he had to turn back. More bad luck prevailed when his ship was driven off-course to Sicily. A long trudge up the foot of Italy followed, until he came to Assisi. Here, he met the great St Francis, and was sent out to a hermitage to practise his devotions.

But it was soon realised that his skills lay more in preaching than in prayer and, before long, he was on the road again, this time to Lombardy in northern Italy. He was small and podgy, but he attracted people to him, so much so that the churches were not big enough to hold all those who wanted to listen, and he was forced to go out to the market place. Many were converted after hearing his ardent words, delivered in a strong and powerful voice.

High offices were offered to him, but he preferred to take his message direct to the people so, instead of opting for glittering apartments in Rome, Antony settled in the small town of Padua, and remained there until his death. It was here that he was to see the fruits of all his labours at the pulpit, with many citizens turning to Christ on his account. He died in 1231, aged only 36, and became a saint the year after.

• Antony of Padua is also patron saint of Lost articles, and of Portugal.

HOUSE-HUNTING

Joseph

Saint day: 19 March

JOSEPH, of course, is the most famous house-hunter in the world. Amid the throngs, in Bethlehem to register for taxes under Augustus Caesar, and with Mary about to give birth, Joseph searched in vain for shelter. They were exhausted, but the city was crowded, and there was no room anywhere, until a kindly inn-keeper, seeing Mary's condition, offered his stable. There Jesus was born.

Joseph provides encouragement, through his patronage, for people searching for a suitable home, though not necessarily in such pressing circumstances.

• Joseph is also patron saint of Carpenters.

INFERTILITY

Rita of Cascia

Saint day: 22 May

R ITA is invoked against infertility because of her parents' advanced age when she was born, in the small mountain village of Roccaborena, Italy, in 1381. In her own life, she was blessed with two sons, but was unhappily married to a brutal man. She had not wanted to wed at all, cherishing an ambition to join the nuns at Cascia, but she bowed to parental pressure and married when just 15. She tried to be a good wife, and stood the beatings and numerous infidelities for 18 years, when it became apparent that her two sons were falling under the spell of their evil father.

Still constant in her faith, despite her unhappy life, Rita prayed for her children's deliverance. As if by a miracle, her husband relented and asked forgiveness for past ill-treatment. A new, happy life seemed to beckon but, shortly afterwards, her husband was brought home dead, with many wounds upon his body. Rita's two sons vowed to avenge the murder, and went out to seek the culprit. But Rita so abhorred violence, however just the cause, that she would rather her own sons die than commit murder. Her prayers to this effect were answered because, before they could mete out rough justice to their father's assailant, the sons died from fatal illnesses.

Now all alone, Rita approached the nunnery at Cascia, but found they took only virgins. Undaunted, she tried

again and again, until the rules were relaxed in her
favour, and she entered in 1413. She was still only 32.
Rita was a perfect example of devotion, and spent the
remaining 44 years of her life ministering to Christians
who were neglecting their faith.

JUSTICE, SOCIAL

Martin of Porres

Saint day: 3 November

IN his role as a lay-brother, in his home town of Lima,
Martin, originally a barber-surgeon, was responsible
for the care of the sick. He did not, however, just minister to those who managed to stagger to his door. He
went out into the teeming city itself, healing as he went.
He also established an orphanage and foundling hospital
for the hundreds of displaced children who were the sad
result of liaisons between the Spanish garrison and local
women.

He even found the time to look out for the welfare of
slaves who had been shipped in from Africa. In fact, any
underprivileged people, whose lot in life was not of their
own doing, were targets for Martin's compassion.

He was so admired that, upon his death in 1639, the
humble barber-surgeon was borne to his grave by
prelates and noblemen. His striving for better conditions
for all led to his canonisation in 1962.

• Martin of Porres is also patron saint of Hairdressers.

Lost Articles

Antony of Padua

Saint day: 13 June

A NTONY of Padua has become the patron saint of lost articles as a result of a curious incident involving a novice Franciscan friar and Antony's own psalter. The psalm book was a thing of value, especially to a friar whose worldly goods were necessarily meagre, and the newcomer borrowed it without permission. He returned it, however, after a fearful apparition had appeared to him, presumably threatening dire consequences if he hung on to property that was not his.

• Antony of Padua is also patron saint of Harvests, and of Portugal.

LOST CAUSES

Jude

Saint day: 28 October

JUDE became patron saint of lost causes because he was seen to be one himself – due to confused identity and guilt by association. His true credentials were good. He was an Apostle – sometimes known as Thaddeus – and the brother of the Apostle James the Less. After the Ascension of Christ, Jude went to Persia with the Apostle Simon the Zealot, where both were martyred for their faith. He is also the author of the *Epistle of Jude* in the *New Testament*.

However, his name resembled too closely that of the betrayer, Judas Iscariot, and so people did not invoke him for help unless they were really desperate – their case had to be hopeless, and all other sources of supplication exhausted, before Jude was called in. Faith in his support is demonstrated, in modern times, in the classified advertisement columns of the London *Times*, where messages of thanks to Jude for assistance with deeply personal problems appear quite frequently.

LOVERS

Valentine

Saint day: 14 February

THE adoption of Valentine as the patron saint of lovers and courting couples is shrouded in the mists of Roman pagan festivals. But there is no doubt that a Valentine existed – maybe even two. One was a Roman priest; the other, a bishop. Both were executed in Rome, but the bishop's bones were taken back to his episcopal seat at Terni. Their fates were so similar, however, that some say both were one and the same person. It certainly seems that one or other, or both, were martyred on 14 February, as this date crops up in the *Roman Martyrology* (an early catalogue of Christian martyrs).

The association with lovers then takes a quantum leap to the same date when, in England at least, birds are said to pair off. At around the same time occurred the Roman feast of Lupercalia, a fertility rite. Both have been combined to make this date the time for love, and Valentine seems to have taken on the patronage by sheer coincidence.

Curiously, no churches are dedicated to him, although his feast has been retained in the Roman calendar, while less contentious claimants have sometimes been dropped.

MARRIAGES, UNHAPPY

Gengulf

Saint day: 11 May

THIS 8th-century knight from Burgundy is known to have worked many miracles, to have been highly respected in the community, and to have been a particular favourite of the regional ruler (he would even sleep in his tent during campaigns). Gengulf was not to be rewarded on this earth, however, for his wife took pleasure in a whole series of extra-marital affairs.

Unwilling to live with such overt infidelity, Gengulf chose to leave her and retreated to a castle at Avallon where he proceeded to live an exemplary life, even providing for his former spouse. Tragically, legend has it that in the year 760, he was cruelly murdered in his bed by one of his wife's lovers.

MOTHERHOOD

Nicholas of Tolentino

Saint day: 10 September

AS far as his middle-aged parents were concerned, the arrival of Nicholas was nothing short of a miracle. Childless for many years, his desperate mother went on a pilgrimage to the shrine of St Nicholas at Myra to plead his intervention with God to grant her a child who, she said, would faithfully serve him.

Her prayers were answered and a son was born in 1245. He was named after his patron, and was entered into minor orders while still only a boy, fulfilling his mother's promise. He has therefore become the patron saint of mothers, as a sign of recognition of his own mother's faith in prayer.

MOTORWAYS

John the Baptist

Saint day: 24 June/29 August

THE coming of John the Baptist as the precursor of Jesus was foretold in the prophecies of Isaiah, which are recorded in the *Old Testament*. When outlining the coming of the Messiah, Isaiah refers to John as being sent directly from God with the express purpose of preparing the people for Jesus' ministry: 'Behold I send my messenger before thy face, who shall prepare thy way; the voice of one crying in the wilderness: Prepare the way of the Lord, make his paths straight.'

This prophecy is taken up in the Gospels of *Matthew*, *Mark* and *Luke*, when introducing John; while the Gospel of *John the Apostle* records the Baptist's own words, in answer to the priests, who demanded he give an account of himself. John says: 'I am the voice of one crying in the wilderness. "Make straight the way of the Lord," as the prophet Isaiah said.'

These 'straight ways' are seen to have something in common with motorways, and so John has been adopted as their patron saint, although this patronage is not yet officially recognised.

• John is also patron saint of Spas, and of Jordan.

NEIGHBOURHOOD WATCH

Sebastian

Saint day: 20 January

SEBASTIAN is fabled to have been a captain in the personal bodyguards of the 4th-century Roman Emperor, Diocletian. But when it was discovered that Sebastian was a Christian, Diocletian ordered him to be shot to death by arrows. This did not work and so, even as Sebastian was berating the emperor for his cruelty, he was beaten lifeless with clubs.

He is usually represented in mediaeval art as a young man, naked and pierced with arrows. But Neighbourhood Watch schemes have adopted him from happier times when it was his duty to keep the Roman emperor safe.

• Sebastian is also patron saint of Archers.

OLD PEOPLE

Teresa of Jornet e Ibars

Saint day: 26 August

TERESA was born in 1843, in Aytona, near Lerida, Spain. She began teaching in her mid-teens, but was soon clear in her ambitions to become a nun. She entered a congregation, founded by her uncle, in 1862, and joined the 'Poor Clares' six years later. This Order was noted for its austere life, and it broke Teresa's health. After four years, she had to leave.

Instead, she joined a congregation at Barbistro, run by a priest, where the emphasis was more on helping others than depriving oneself. The priest was particularly concerned with the elderly poor, who often had nowhere to go. He opened up his own house at first, but bought a special property to house them when their numbers became too great for his modest abode.

Teresa was in charge of the new hostel, and took on other women helpers. This new congregation was known as the 'Little Sisters of the Abandoned Old'. The helpers were not nuns, but lay women dedicated to easing the last years of their charges. The congregation had been going a little over 20 years, when it received papal approval, in 1897, the year Teresa died.

Since then, branches of the 'Little Sisters' have been established as far afield as Cuba, Puerto Rico, and Colombia in South America, while Teresa herself was canonised in 1974.

ORPHANS

Jerome Emiliani

Saint day: 8 February

JEROME Emiliani began life in Venice in 1481, becoming an officer in the Venetian army upon reaching adulthood. He was captured during one campaign, but managed to escape. By his late twenties, Jerome had renounced the military life for the priesthood, to which he was ordained in 1518.

After surviving a bout of plague in 1531, Jerome devoted his life entirely to the relief of suffering, founding hospitals, orphanages and houses for repentant prostitutes. But it was the orphans who were closest to his heart, and he made it his business to see that all who came into his care were properly educated, so that they could take their place in society.

Jerome died in 1537, aged 56, and became a saint in 1767. He was declared patron saint of orphans by Pope Pius XI in 1928.

PETS

Antony the Abbot

Saint day: 17 January

A MERCHANT'S son from Coma (Upper Egypt),
Antony gave up his worldly goods and lived much
of his life in solitude, often in the desert, where no man
came to visit him, save to deliver food. Even though he
was prevailed upon, several times, to leave his hermitage – to found a monastery, to fortify the courage of
Christians under persecution in Alexandria, and to argue
the meaning of Christianity – Antony always returned
to the solitary life.

After his death in 356, no one knew where he was
buried until his bones were discovered in 561, when
they were taken to Alexandria. They were moved again,
some say to La Motte in France where, in the year 1100,
an Order was founded in his name to treat sufferers of
skin disease. The healers wore black robes and used to
ride about, ringing bells to call people to give alms.
These bells were often hung round the necks of animals,
and from this comes Antony's adoption as patron saint
of pets.

Curiously, one of the Order's privileges was that their
pigs were allowed to roam freely (whereas, presumably,
other townsfolks' hogs could not). Although Antony was
long dead by then, he is often depicted accompanied by
pigs and bells.

Pilgrims

Nicholas of Bari

Saint day: 6 December

NICHOLAS has been one of the most popular saints in the Christian world almost since his death in the 4th century. He lived and died in Myra, Turkey, where he was bishop. When the town was taken over by Saracens some 600 years later, several cities saw this as an opportunity to claim the bones for themselves.

Venice and Bari, in Italy, emerged as the frontrunners, but Bari stole a march on the Italian state by spiriting the relics away before anyone knew about it. In 1087, a splendid cathedral was built to house the relics, and Pope Urban II held a council there to celebrate the inauguration in 1095. Soon, the cathedral became a place of pilgrimage to thousands.

• Nicholas of Bari is also patron saint of Brides, Children, Pawnbrokers, Sailors, Unmarried women, Business people, and of Russia.

POSTAL SERVICES

Gabriel

Saint day: 29 September

GABRIEL is celebrated in the Bible as the Archangel who brought the news to Mary of her role as mother to the Son of God. He further appeared to Joseph in a dream to warn him to flee Herod's soldiers who were slaughtering all the baby boys in Bethlehem in an effort to kill Jesus.

As the bearer of news, Gabriel is well-placed to act as patron saint of all means of communication which, of course, includes the postal service. He was recognised as such by Pope Pius XII in 1951.

• Gabriel is also patron saint of Philatelists.

RACE RELATIONS

Peter Claver

Saint day: 9 September

PETER Claver's mission in life was to bring to African slaves a dignity and sense of worth. At the time of his birth, in Catalonia, Spain, in 1580, his country's colonies in Latin America were making money to an astonishing degree. Much of this was in gold and precious metals, mined from the rich earth. The Spaniards had already found that the local Indians were not up to the hard physical work involved, and so they brought slaves from Africa.

A flourishing trade was in existence when Peter Claver set his heart on missionary work, amongst the slaves, in 1600. He joined the Jesuits and, after 10 years' study and preparation, sailed for the New World in 1610. He arrived in the sea port of Cartagena, now in Colombia, to find the conditions for slaves so appalling that he set to work straight away.

He brought fresh food for the survivors, and baptised those on the point of death and babies born on the voyage. Only then did he set about converting the slaves to Christianity. He was very methodical, teaching only small groups at a time, and was fortunate in having a band of interpreters who could speak most of the dialects they came across. During the 40 years of his ministry, Peter converted and baptised over 300,000 slaves. Once they had been sold, he also made it his business to follow up on their welfare.

Peter was 70 years old when he contracted the plague during an epidemic in the city. He was brought back from death's door by careful nursing, but his health was broken. He lived the remaining four years of his life as a recluse, forgotten by almost all of the people he had helped over the years. Only on his death, in 1654, was he recognised as a great man, and given a civic funeral.

• Peter Claver is also patron saint of Peru.

Savings Banks

Anthony Claret

Saint day: 24 October

KNOWN for his many outstanding miracles and prophecies, as well as for founding schools and delivering some 10,000 sermons, Anthony Claret was canonised in 1950.

Born in 1807 in Sallent, northern Spain, he was ordained as a priest and planned to devote his life to missionary work abroad. Ill-health, however, brought him back to Spain, where he went on to found the Missionary Sons of the Immaculate Heart of Mary, known for charitable works.

Later appointed Archbishop of Santiago de Cuba, he set up a savings bank with several branches, specifically designed to help the poor of Santiago – hence his patronage. There were a number attempts on his life; and finally, following exile from Spain with Isabella II (to whom he was confessor), he lived principally in Rome.

SKIERS

Our Lady of Graces

Saint day: 9 June

THE Blessed Virgin Mary is represented as Our Lady of Grace in many shrines around the world, but especially in Italy. Skiers, in particular, have long paid devotion to the statue at a church in Folgaria, in the Italian Alps, before ascending the slopes. In an Apostolic Letter of 1955, Pope Pius XII refers to this custom and declared Our Lady of Graces to be patron saint of all Italian skiers. This has, by custom and practice, extended to skiers worldwide.

• Skiers also have Bernard as their patron saint.

TELEVISION

Clare

Saint day: 11 August

CLARE came from a well-to-do family from Assisi and decided to devote herself to Christ at the age of 18 in the year 1211. She was taken in by St Francis, eventually founding her own Order of Minoresses or Poor Clares. She declined to own property, even making it a rule of her Order that none should be held, but that they must beg for all their daily needs.

She never left her cell at Assisi, but though bedridden for many years until her death, at the age of 60, in 1253, lived to see several foundations of her Order set up in various European countries. She was also well-known for her needlework and embroidery, used to decorate altar cloths.

Always popular throughout the Middle Ages, Clare has taken her place in modern times by being named the patron saint of television. This adoption was sanctioned by Pope Pius XII in 1958 as a result of his awareness of the dangers as well as the benefits of global television. He chose Clare because, one Christmas, when she was unable to rise from her sickbed to attend services, she had a vision of the crib, and could hear the singing in the church, as if she were really present.

• Clare is also patron saint of Embroiderers.

THEFT

Dismas

Saint day: 25 March

DISMAS was one of the two thieves who were crucified on either side of Jesus at Calvary. While his companion sneered at Jesus and challenged him to use his powers to free them all from crucifixion, Dismas simply asked: 'Lord, remember me when you come into your kingdom', to which Jesus replied: 'Today, you will be with me in Paradise.'

This promise was seen as forgiveness for Dismas' sins, and therefore made him eligible for sainthood. From the Middle Ages, Dismas came to be regarded as mentor for thieves and also prisoners, presumably in the hope that they, too, will renounce their wicked ways.

TRAVELLERS

Christopher

Saint day: 25 July

CHRISTOPHER has been associated with travellers from earliest times – depictions of him on mediaeval church walls were always opposite the porch so that passers-by could look on them and be fortified.

The only record of his existence is his death in Asia Minor some time in the 3rd century. Certainly, he was well-known enough as a saint by the 5th century for churches to be dedicated to him. He features in early legends as a Canaanite, a giant of terrifying appearance, who first decided to serve the Devil. But when he found out the Devil was afraid of the Cross, he switched allegiance and followed Christ instead. His name, meaning 'Christ-bearer', fostered the legend of Christopher the hermit, who lived by a river and existed on donations from people he carried across its fast water. One day, a child asked him for help. His burden turned out to be unexpectedly heavy and Christopher was bent double with the weight.

On reaching the other side, the child revealed himself to be Jesus and the weight, symbolically, was that of the world. To signify the truth of his revelations, Jesus told Christopher to plant his staff in the ground and it would flourish. The rod duly sprouted leaves the next day.

Popular depictions are crammed with all these images – bent man, child on his back, raging river and flowering stick. Modern faith in his ability to protect while travelling is shown by the wearing of a St Christopher medallion around the neck, a common practice.

WIDOWS

Frances of Rome

Saint day: 9 March

FRANCES became patron saint of widows for the devotion she showed her husband during 40 years of marriage – a marriage she entered into reluctantly at the age of 13, when she had already decided she would rather become a nun. Her wealthy family, minor Roman nobility, had refused point-blank to allow her to enter Holy Orders, having arranged for her a marriage to one Lorenzo Ponziano, the son of a similarly wealthy family.

Frances resigned herself to her new life, trying her best to be a successful wife, but all the while keeping up her original desire to serve God by visiting the poor and sick during her spare time. She was particularly known for her visits to the hospital of Santo Spirito in Sassia.

Dressed in plain clothes, she singled out sufferers from the worst diseases and cared for them.

The devoted Lorenzo encouraged his wife's ministrations, which she continued during the upbringing of her three children. Frances' life of perfect compromise came to an abrupt end in 1408 when troops loyal to the antipope (it was the time of the Great Schism when Christianity was divided over its beliefs) overran Rome, burning homes as they went. The Ponziano household suffered like the rest, but Frances continued to live in the ruins, caring for her even poorer neighbours.

Tragically, two of her children died when in their teens, but Frances soldiered on. She even founded a community of like-minded wives, called the Oblates of Tor de' Specchi, where she spent as much time as her domestic duties would allow. When Lorenzo died, she went to live at the Oblate full-time. She spent the last years of her life as a suppliant to her own foundation, thus realising her childhood hope. Frances died in 1440, and was canonised in 1608.

HEALTH AND DISEASE

CHRIST spent much of his ministry healing the sick and dying. Health problems and prayers for protection against them, therefore, figure prominently in Christian life. Indeed, the Church has a pantheon of saints who are invoked to protect against a whole spectrum of diseases. Our selection of maladies shows there may be any one of many reasons for an individual association. A saint may have come into contact with a particular affliction; have contracted and overcome it; or have worked with and ministered to sufferers of it. Alternatively, unexplained cures from a potential disease may have been reported by sufferers who prayed at the saint's shrine. There are certainly many who claim to have found not only the inner strength to combat illness, but also sometimes a cure by praying for the support of the saint assigned to a particular condition.

ABDOMINAL PAINS

Erasmus (Elmo)

Saint day: 2 June

E RASMUS came to represent the interests of people, especially children, with abdominal or colic pains via a gruesome legend concerning his martyrdom. He was a bishop of Formiae, in the Campagna region of Italy, in the late 3rd century, and is said to have been disembowelled for his faith, after suffering several equally nasty attempts by his Roman persecutors to remove him from the planet.

These included being beaten, then rolled in pitch and set on fire. When he somehow survived this, he was thrown into prison while the more effective method of despatch was thought up. His crimes were to be a Christian and a bishop, who managed to escape the persecutions of the Roman Emperor, Diocletian, in the early 4th century by hiding out as a hermit on Mount Lebanon, but he was discovered eventually.

• Erasmus is also patron saint of Sailors.

BLINDNESS

Cosmas and Damian

Saint day: 26 September

THESE two early Christian surgeons forged a reputation for asking no fees of the poor. It is not known when they lived, but a basilica was built in Cyrrhus, Asia Minor, in recognition of their martyrdom there; and other dedicated churches, in Rome and Constantinople, exist from the 5th century.

They are thought to have been pioneers of eye surgery, so that success in alleviating blindness led to them becoming patron saints for that affliction, too.

• Cosmas and Damian are also patron saints of Surgeons.

BLOOD DONORS

Our Lady of the Thorns

Saint day: none

THIS is the title of an image of the Blessed Virgin Mary, which is venerated at Sissa, in the diocese of Parma, Italy. As blood donors in the area made a habit of praying at the shrine, Our Lady of Thorns was sanctioned as patron of blood donors everywhere by the Pope in 1981.

BREASTFEEDING

Basilissa the Martyr

Saint day: 3 September

VERY little is known about Basilissa, except that she lived in the 3rd-century Roman Empire. She was only nine years old when her persecutors, unable to shake her from her Christian faith, had her stripped, beaten and thrown to two lions who tore her to pieces.

Her cult flourished in mediaeval Europe, especially in Constantinople in the 14th century. However, it is not known why she was adopted as the patron saint for breastfeeding.

• Basilissa is also venerated as patron saint of Chilblains.

CANCER SUFFERERS

Peregrine Laziosi

Saint day: 1 May

CANCER must have been feared in mediaeval times far more than today, on account of there being no cure – except, when possible, amputation. So it was that Peregrine's miraculous cure of the cancer in his foot inspired those who came after him to invoke him to work similar cures upon their own afflictions.

Peregrine was born in 1260, the son of a wealthy Italian merchant. There was a lot of anti-papal feeling in the town at the time, and he became involved in the harassment of clerics. During one riot, which the Pope's envoy, St Philip Benizi, had come to quell, Peregrine roughed-up the saint and struck him on the face. When St Philip, literally, turned the other cheek, Peregrine held back, resolving to follow Christ.

One day, the Virgin Mary appeared to him while he was at prayer and urged him to go to Siena, which he did, and where he was ordained priest. He went home to found a religious house, but soon developed cancer of the foot. The night before surgeons were to amputate – without anaesthetic in those days of course – Peregrine spent many hours in prayer before falling into a light sleep. On awakening, he found the cancer had gone. Peregrine lived to the age of 85, and was canonised in 1726.

CONTAGIOUS DISEASES

Sebastian

Saint day: 20 January

SEBASTIAN joined the Roman army in about 283, and was assigned to guard the Emperor Diocletian. When the Roman ruler began persecuting the Christians, Sebastian, by now a follower of Christ himself, gave comfort to fellow believers when they were imprisoned.

It was only a matter of time before he, too, was discovered, and Diocletian, enraged that one so close to him should have turned to the religion he was trying to stamp out, ordered that Sebastian be shot to death with arrows. When this failed, and Sebastian berated Diocletian for his cruelty, the brave soldier was beaten to death with clubs.

During his lifetime, Sebastian was said to have the power to cure the plague and, as such, was nominated as patron saint for all contagious diseases. His martyrdom, by so many arrow wounds, has also been invoked as the reason for his special powers: the arrow points are said to have had an immunising effect against pestilence.

118

FEVER

Genevieve

Saint day: 3 January

GENEVIEVE was born in France in the year 422 and, from a very early age – seven years old – decided on a life of devotion. Accordingly, she took the veil when only 15 and began a life of austerity. She ate only twice a week, her meal consisting of barley-bread and beans.

Although she spent best part of her time in prayer, Genevieve was not averse to taking action when necessary. When the Frankish king Childeric laid siege to Paris, she led a band of armed men out of the city and brought back boatloads of provisions for the starving people. It is likely her patronage of fever sufferers stems from this, as disease would have been rife in the stricken city. Her brave forays for food helped the people to survive and thereby fight off infection.

• Genevieve is also patron saint of Disasters.

HEADACHES

Denis, Bishop of Paris

Saint day: 9 October

Denis is thought to have become the patron saint of headaches due to being beheaded as a martyr in 3rd-century Gaul (France). Italian by birth, he and four other bishops were sent to Gaul to convert the pagans. He settled in Paris and preached with such success that he was able to establish a Christian centre there, on an island in the middle of the River Seine.

Somewhere along the way, he got on the wrong side of the pagan rulers of Gaul, and was imprisoned with two companions. They all suffered death by decapitation at a place which became known as the 'Hill of Martyrs' (now the Parisian artists' colony called Montmartre), and their bodies were thrown into the river. Faithful followers retrieved the remains and buried them under what is now the Cathedral of Saint Denis in Paris.

• Denis is also patron saint of France.

HERNIAS

Cathal (Catald)

Saint day: 10 May

A s many of his countrymen had done before him, the 7th-century Irish monk, Cathal, chose exile to demonstrate his allegiance to Christ and crossed the sea to Europe, ending up in Italy. Not much is known about Cathal's everyday works, but he seems to have had the power to control a wide variety of afflictions, and was sufficiently admired for his likeness to be incorporated into the basilica of the Nativity at Bethlehem.

He died and was buried at Taranto, in the south of the country, in about 685, but his tomb was not discovered until the 11th century. Devotion to Cathal spread through mediaeval Italy and across the Mediterranean to Sicily and Malta, where a 'catacomb of St Cathal' is frequented by local hernia sufferers.

• Cathal is also invoked against Plague, Drought and Storms, although the reasons for these particular associations are not known.

121

HOARSENESS

Bernardino of Siena

Saint day: 20 May

BERNARDINO is invoked to help people who have lost their voices because he suffered from the same symptoms himself throughout his life as one of the 14th century's finest preachers.

He was born in Massa, Italy, the son of the city governor, in 1381. Bernardino lost both his parents while still very young and, as soon as he was old enough, entered the local order of Franciscan friars. He remained cloistered for 12 years but, at the age of 36, was sent out to preach. Bernardino did not have a natural gift for projecting his voice, and often dried up altogether through the sheer effort of shouting. However, he endured many hours of vocal exercises to strengthen his delivery. Perseverance paid off, as his voice became loud and clear, and he won many souls to Christ.

• Bernardino is also patron saint of Advertising executives and Public relations personnel.

HYDROPHOBIA (RABIES)

Hubert

Saint day: 30 May

H UBERT is said to have been the son of the French Duke of Guienne. As a pagan, Good Friday meant nothing to him, and he went out hunting as usual. He was about to kill a stag, when a vision of the crucified Christ appeared between its antlers. Hubert dropped his sword and became a Christian there and then.

He went on to become Bishop of Maastricht, in 705, and then Liège, where he also built a cathedral to house the relics of St Lambert, his predecessor at Maastricht. He died in about 727, and his remains were taken to what is now called St Hubert, in Belgium, in 743.

Hubert is depicted in art accompanied by a book with a stag on its cover, or with the stag itself lying at his feet. A hunting horn, which was supposed to have been his, is held by the Wallace Collection in London.

As a huntsman, Hubert would have kept dogs and was therefore exposed to dog bites from which rabies is contracted. A legend also tells that he was given a white and gold scarf by the Blessed Virgin Mary. Sufferers from rabies at the time were treated by having a thread from the scarf applied to an incision on their forehead.

• Hubert is the patron saint of Hunting, too, while Ubald of Gubbio is also invoked against Rabies.

LAMENESS

Giles

Saint day: 1 September

GILES was a 7th-century hermit who lived in southern France and who, apparently, had an exceptional rapport with animals.

One day, a hind, breathless from the chase, came to him for protection. Her pursuer was the local king, called Wamba, who promptly tried his luck at bringing her down with an arrow. Instead, he hit Giles, wounding and crippling him. Whether or not it was out of remorse for this affront, Wamba gave Giles land on which he built a monastery.

Giles' own suffering and protection of the hind have made him the hope of crippled people, lepers and nursing mothers alike. Hospitals as well as churches have been named after him – none so apt, perhaps, as St Giles Hospital in *Cripplegate*, London.

MENTAL ILLNESS

Dympna

Saint day: 15 May

THE mentally ill of Dympna's adopted town of Gheel, near Antwerp, Belgium, were miraculously cured of their afflictions when her bones were moved 600 years after her death. Ever since, the town has had an exemplary reputation for its work with sufferers of many forms of mental disorder.

Legend has it that she was the daughter of a 7th-century Celtic king. Her mother died when she was only a child and, as Dympna grew up, her father saw that she bore an uncanny resemblance to his dead wife. He fell in love with his daughter who, realising the awful implications, escaped with her confessor, St Gerebernus, to Antwerp, from where she travelled to the town of Gheel, 25 miles further on, settling there.

Her father was soon in hot pursuit, tracing them by coins of his realm that they had spent along the way on food. When Dympna refused to go back with him, he had her killed, together with her confessor. She was buried where she fell, but her bones were finally laid to rest in a more fitting place in Gheel.

• Dympna is also patron saint of Epilepsy, because of outdated associations with mental illness.

Skin Diseases

Marculf

Saint day: 1 May

Marculf's influence in halting the ravages of skin diseases extended beyond his own intervention, at least in France, the country of his birth in 558. For centuries, kings on their coronation day proceeded from the cathedral at Rheims to venerate his relics at Corbény. During the service, Marculf's healing influence passed to the king, or so it was said, and thereafter, the new monarch could heal scrofula. Indeed, the disease was known as 'The King's Evil'. This practice died out in more enlightened times, and came to an abrupt end, as did the French monarchy, in the Revolution of 1789. Marculf, himself, however, continues to hold sway over skin afflictions, nearly 1500 years after his death.

His mission was to convert pagans, still in the majority in 6th-century Gaul. He was very successful, but his heart was not in it. He preferred the contemplative life, away from the mass of humanity, and often used to retire to a lonely island for its solitude. Eventually, he was given a piece of land at Nanteuil, on which he built frugal huts for himself and a few like-minded disciples.

In Nanteuil, the few soon grew to many and, in no time, Marculf had a great monastery about him. He gave up the idea of complete solitude, became the first abbot, and was finally buried there in 558.

SPAS

John the Baptist

Saint day: 24 June/29 August

SPAS have taken as their patron saint the man who used the waters of the Jordan river to wash away sins. John the Baptist was born six months before Jesus, to a kinswoman of Mary. Little is known of his life until the time came for him to pave the way for the Messiah.

Then, he went out into the desert, lived on locusts and wild honey, and clothed himself in animal skins. He probably had an untrimmed beard and uncombed hair, and presented a completely different picture of a preacher from the smooth, well-dressed priests of the Temple. People were curious and flocked to hear his message. They stayed and were baptized. When the time came for him to begin his ministry, Jesus himself came for baptism.

Spas had been visited long before Roman times – there was a 'healing pool' in Jerusalem – by people wishing to improve their health. Contemporaries of John the Baptist, therefore, would have been familiar with the notion of healing through the administration of water. That he chose the muddy waters of the Jordan and spoke of spiritual healing probably puzzled them at first, before they heeded his message.

• John is also patron saint of Motorways, and of Jordan.

TOOTHACHE

Apollonia

Saint day: 9 February

APOLLONIA lived in 4th-century Alexandria where she fell victim to the persecutions. She refused to give up her Christianity, and was sentenced to death. Her martyrdom began when she had her teeth smashed. Other legends depict torturers extracting her teeth with pincers. At all events, the trial was very painful, but she lived through it, only to be burned at the stake.

• By association, Apollonia is also patron saint of Dentists.

VENEREAL DISEASES

Fiacre

Saint day: 1 September

FIACRE was born in Ireland early in the 7th century. As one who chose 'exile for Christ', he left his homeland and travelled to France, settling in the small town of Meaux. The bishop, St Faro, gave him land on which Fiacre built a hermitage, living out his life there until death, from natural causes, in about the year 670.

Fiacre has been invoked as patron saint of venereal disease because of his legendary hatred of women – said to extend beyond the grave – although this seems to indicate he favours male sufferers, who may have reason to detest the sex who could have put them in that position, rather than women who can, of course, also catch the disease from men.

• Fiacre is also the patron saint of Taxi drivers.

WOMEN IN LABOUR

Anne

Saint day: 26 July

ANNE was the mother of Mary, chosen by God to bear his son, Jesus, so he could appear on Earth in fleshy form. Although none of the Gospels in the *New Testament* make any mention of her at all at the Nativity, a legend grew up of her presence there from the apocryphal *Gospel of James the Apostle*. Certainly, this possibility bore credence right up to Renaissance times, when Leonardo da Vinci sketched out his famous cartoon – now in the National Gallery, London – in which he included Anne with the Holy Family.

Throughout the early centuries, shrines to Anne proliferated, especially in Constantinople and Rome, while she was worshipped as a saint in England from about 1100. If she had been at the Nativity, then it would have been her role to help Mary through what would have been a difficult labour, in a draughty stable on a winter's night. Consequently, as the helper at the most important birth in Christendom, Anne has since been patron saint of all women in labour.

In art, she is often represented teaching Mary to read, and sometimes with her husband, Joachim, at their betrothal.

PATRON SAINTS
WORLDWIDE

THE following list features countries and regions in all five continents boasting one or more patron saints. Roughly half of these have chosen a saint who once lived there; a bishop or ruler who brought Christianity to the land; a subject whose good works have earned him or her a special place in Heaven; an Apostle who has a connection with that country; or even a national hero unconnected with the Church. The remaining countries have adopted the Blessed Virgin Mary, celebrating an event in her life, or her appearance at a particular place in the country where a shrine is established. Read on to find out which saint (or saints) looks out for your country, one to which you may be travelling, or where you have family and friends.

Africa – North	**Cyprian, Bishop of Carthage** (16 September): 3rd-century bishop, born in Carthage. Executed in 258 during the persecutions of the Roman Emperor, Valerian.
Africa – Central	**Blessed Virgin Mary – The Most Pure Heart of Mary** (22 August): Chosen because of the devotion to the immaculate nature of Mary by 17th- and 19th-century missionaries.
Albania	**Blessed Virgin Mary – Motherhood of Good Counsel** (26 April): Likeness of Mary under this title discovered in early Middle Ages, balanced on a narrow ledge in mountains near Gennazzano, south-east of Rome. Seemed to be held in place by miraculous force – even bombs dropped during World War II failed to dislodge it. Many miracles associated with it. Veneration of Mary under this name practised in Skodra, Albania, even before the icon appeared at Gennazzano.
Algeria	**Cyprian, Bishop of Carthage**: SEE *Africa – North*.
Angola	**Blessed Virgin Mary – Immaculate Heart** (22 August): Another name for the Most Pure Heart. SEE *Africa – Central* and *Ecuador*.
Arabia	**Blessed Virgin Mary – Our Lady of Arabia** (8 December): Statue of Mary, housed in a church at Ahmadi, was blessed by the Pope in 1950, and became a focus of devotion for Christian oilmen from many nations. The day designated for celebration is the Feast of the Immaculate Conception.

Argentina **Blessed Virgin Mary – Our Lady of Lujan** (Saturday preceding the fourth Sunday after Easter): A 17th-century icon of Mary was left at Lujan and a local landowner built a shrine for it. The icon was designated patron saint of Argentina in 1930, the 300th anniversary of its arrival at Lujan.

Armenia **Gregory of Armenia** (16 March): 10th-century monk who became bishop of Nikopolis, in Armenia, suffered persecution and fled to France, where he ended his days as a hermit in Pithiviers, near Orléans.

Australia **Blessed Virgin Mary – Our Lady of Help of Christians** (24 May): Early missionaries to Australia and New Zealand, from the Society of Mary – known as Marists – venerated Mary under this title.

Austria **Joseph** (19 March): Husband of Mary, mother of Jesus.

Coloman (13 October): 11th-century Scot who was crossing Austria on a pilgrimage to Jerusalem, when he was stopped at Stockrau on suspicion of being a spy for enemies of Austria, and hanged. Canonization granted because patience under unjust suffering taken as proof of sanctity.

Leopold (15 November): 12th-century bishop and founder of several religious houses, who consolidated Christianity in Austria. Offered crown in 1125, but refused.

Florian (4 November): 3rd-century Christian officer in the Roman army, who held a high post at Noricum, now part of Austria. Suffered persecution under the Emperor Diocletian and executed at Lorch by drowning.

Barbados **Andrew, the Apostle** (30 November): Feast day coincides with National Day.

Belgium **Blessed Virgin Mary**

Joseph (19 March): Husband of Mary, mother of Jesus.

Belize **Joseph** (19 March): Husband of Mary, mother of Jesus.

Bolivia **Blessed Virgin Mary – Our Lady of Mount Carmel** (16 July): Statue housed in a church of the Order of Mount Carmel, now in Israel, represents a vision of Mary by the English saint, Simon Stock, who reorganised the 12th-century Order in 1251. In 1674, permission sought from the Pope to celebrate the Feast in Spain and all her dominions which, at the time, included Bolivia.

Borneo **Francis Xavier** (3 December): 16th-century Spanish priest and co-founder, with Ignatius Loyola, of the Society of Jesus (Jesuits). Travelled to the East Indies, India, Ceylon and Malaysia to Christianize the populations. Also visited Japan, making 2,000 converts, and on way to China when he died, at San-chian Island, in 1552.

Brazil

Blessed Virgin Mary – Immaculate 'Aparecida' (11 May): A statue of Mary, carved out of black wood, was found by fishermen in a river near Sao Paolo in 1717, and became an object of devotion. Aparecida – 'she who appeared' – was confirmed as patron saint of Brazil in 1930.

Peter of Alcantara (11 October): 16th-century Spanish mystic and Franciscan monk, who founded monastery at Badajoz when only 22. Eventually became a hermit in Alcantara, Portugal, where joined by like-minded men and founded the Order of Alcantrines. Renowned for his austerity. Canonized in 1669 and named patron saint of Brazil the same year.

Canada

Joseph (19 March): Husband of Mary, mother of Jesus.

Martyrs of North America (19 October): Principally Jean Brebeuf, a French Jesuit priest sent to Canada in 1625 to Christianize the Huron Indians. Murdered by their enemies, the Iroquois, in 1649. Fellow Jesuit, Isaac Jogues, was enslaved by the Iroquois, but escaped to France. On his return, captured and killed by the Mohawk, in 1646.

Canary Islands

Avitus (27 January): Brought Christianity to the islands and became their first bishop. Martyred in Africa.

Central America

Rose of Lima (23 August): 16th-century Peruvian recluse who lived exemplary life and died at the early age of 31. Patronage of Peru declared in 1670 and extended to Central America a few years later.

Chile   **Blessed Virgin Mary – Our Lady of Mount Carmel** (16 July). SEE *Bolivia*.

China   **Blessed Virgin Mary – Queen of China:** The title hails from the days of the missionaries to China, whose devotions centred round Mary as Queen of Heaven. Mary confirmed as patron saint under this title in 1941.

Joseph (19 March): Husband of Mary, mother of Jesus.

Colombia **Blessed Virgin Mary – Our Lady of Chiquinquira** (18 November): In 1586, a new image of Mary appeared on the canvas of a tattered painting, housed in the chapel belonging to Antonio de Santana at Chiquinquira, high in the Andes, while his cousin was praying there. Icon confirmed as patron saint in 1962.

Louis Betrand (9 October): 16th-century Spanish Dominican friar sent to Cartagena, Colombia, to Christianize the Indians. Six-year mission was hugely successful. He returned to Spain, where he died in 1581.

Peter Claver (9 September): Missionary to African slaves at Cartagena.

Corsica   **Blessed Virgin Mary – Immaculate Conception** (8 December): Feast celebrating Mary's freedom from sin at her conception.

Devota (27 January): A native of Corsica, executed on the rack in 303, during persecutions of the Roman Emperor Diocletian, while still only a young girl. Relics survive at the Riviera di Porienti in Monaco.

Julia (22 May): 5th-century Christian from noble family in Carthage, North Africa, sold into slavery by invading vandals and put on ship to Gaul. On stopover in Corsica, Julia refused to join in pagan festival, and nailed to a cross.

Costa Rica   **Blessed Virgin Mary – Our Lady of the Angels** (2 August): Icon is statue of Mary holding Jesus, found by old Indian near city of Cartago on 2 August, 1646. When he tried to move it, the statue returned to its original position. Icon was so called because it was found on the Feast Day of St Mary of the Angels. Confirmed as patron saint in 1914.

Cuba   **Blessed Virgin Mary – The Birthday of The Blessed Virgin of Charity** (8 September): Associated with statue of Mary, left behind in Indian village as offering by Spanish *Conquistadores*, in 1508. After Cuba won independence from Spain in 19th century, the army petitioned the Pope to name the Feast Day of Mary's birth as patron saint.

Cyprus   **Barnabas, the Apostle** (11 June): Given title 'Apostle' by St Luke, but not one of twelve chosen by Christ. A Cypriot Jew, he is first mentioned in the *Acts of the Apostles*, looking after converts in Jerusalem. Joined St Paul in his mission to Antioch, and afterwards brought Christianity to Cyprus.

Czech Republic/ Bohemia and Slovak Republic

Wenceslaus (28 September): 10th-century Duke of Bohemia who became King in 922, at age of fifteen.His support of newly founded Christian Church led to bitter pagan opposition, and he was murderedfollowing a plot involving his brother, Boleslav. He is the 'Wenceslas' made famous by the Christmas carol, although deeds recounted there have no basis in fact.

Adalbert of Prague (23 April): Born in 956, Adalbert was the first native bishop of Prague, then capital of Bohemia. Encountered great opposition from pagans and lapsed Christians, and twice fled to Rome. On his second return, sent to Prussia, where murdered in 997. Body thrown into the Baltic Sea and washed up in Poland. Credited with founding first monasteries in north-east Europe.

John Nepomucen (16 May): Vicar-general of Prague about 1380, who quarrelled with King Wenceslaus IV and was executed by drowning in the River Moldau.

Cyril & Methodius (14 February): Greek-born brothers who were great scholars in Constantinople before becoming monks. Sent to the Slavonic lands in south-east Europe, to Christianize the people, using their own Slavonic language. The 'cyrillic' alphabet, now used in Russia, Serbia and Bulgaria, is attributed to Cyril's followers.

Denmark   **Anskar** (3 February): 9th-century, French-born Bishop of Bremen, Germany, invited by the Danish King Harold to Christianize his people in about 830. Anskar eventually returned to Bremen, where he died in 865.

Dominican Republic   **Blessed Virgin Mary – Our Lady of Mercy** (24 September): This is the title of a 13th-century image of Mary, with her cloak outstretched to cover those who seek help, and also the name of a Spanish religious order – known as the Mercedarians, founded in 1220 to rescue Christians taken as slaves by the Moors. As a former Spanish possession, the Dominican Republic also venerated Mary under this title, chosen by President Garcia Moreno as the country's patron saint, in 1875.

Ecuador   **Blessed Virgin Mary – The Most Pure Heart of Mary** (22 August). SEE *Africa – Central* and *Angola*.

Egypt   **Mark, the Evangelist** (25 April): Author of the second New Testament Gospel, and identified as John Mark, whose mother's house in Jerusalem was a meeting place for the Apostles. Traditionally claimed as first bishop of Alexandria, where he founded the Egyptian Coptic Church. Relics were taken to Venice, of which he is also patron saint, and rest in the Basilica of St Mark.

El Salvador   **Blessed Virgin Mary – Our Lady of Peace** (21 November): A statue of Mary, holding an olive branch, now resides in the church of St Michael in the capital, San Salvador, after – legend has it – rescued from a shipwreck. Mary's intercession is believed to have saved the city from an erupting volcano in 1787. Statue also regarded as image of peace in the war of independence.

Salvador del Mundo (6 August): In Spanish, this title means the saviour of the world – that is, Jesus Christ. The country and capital city take their name from this reference.

England	**George** (23 April): 4th-century soldier-saint adopted by Richard the Lionheart (1189-99) during the Crusades.
Equatorial Guinea	**Blessed Virgin Mary – Immaculate Conception** (8 December): Feast celebrating Mary's freedom from sin at her conception.
Europe	**Benedict** (11 July): Fifth-century monk regarded as the father of monasticism in Europe.
Finland	**Henry the Emperor** (19 January): English-born Papal Legate to Scandinavia, who accompanied Swedish King Eric IV in a war to repel invaders from Finland in 1154. Sweden's victory led him to have power over the Finns, whom he brought to Christianity. Stayed to continue missionary work, but was murdered in 1156.
France	**Blessed Virgin Mary – The Assumption** (15 August): Feast celebrating Mary's bodily assumption into heaven at her death.

Joan of Arc (30 May): French peasant girl, born in 1412 and brought up during the Hundred Years' War between England and France. After hearing voices, at the age of fourteen, telling her to 'Save France', she persuaded the French Dauphin (Crown Prince) to allow her to lead the French armies. Famous victories ensued, notably the relief of Orléans in 1429. Leading clerics, jealous of her success, plotted to have her branded a heretic, and sold her to the English, who burned her at the stake in 1431.

Denis (9 October): 3rd-century Italian missionary to Gaul (France) and first bishop of Paris. Executed during the persecution of Christians by Roman Emperor Valerian.

Thérèse of Lisieux (1 October): Carmelite nun, born in 1873, whose exemplary life, spiritual autobiography, *The Story of a Soul,* and early death from tuberculosis at the age of 24 began a cult which spread all over France, of which she became third patron saint in 1947.

Germany

Anskar (3 February): Bishop of Bremen. SEE *Denmark*.

Michael, the Archangel (29 September): One of three archangels mentioned in the Bible. Credited with great power in Heaven and renowned as a law-giver.

Gibraltar

Bernard of Clairvaux (20 August): 12th-century nobleman from Burgundy who became a monk and revived the Cistercian Order of monasteries in France. Went on to found the monastery at Clairvaux and 68 other monasteries throughout Europe.

Greece　**Paul, the Apostle** (29 June): Originally a Jew called Saul, he persecuted Christians until had vision of Jesus on the road to Damascus. Became a great missionary whose life is recorded in the New Testament *Acts of the Apostles.* Also author of several Epistles to fledgling churches in and around Palestine and Asia Minor. Missionary expeditions included Greece and Cyprus. On way to trial in Rome (as a Roman citizen) after arrest in Jerusalem, shipwrecked on Malta where imprisoned for two years. Eventually, beheaded with St Peter during persecutions of Emperor Nero in 65.

George (23 April): 4th-century soldier-saint.

Guatemala　**James the Greater, the Apostle** (25 July): One of the twelve disciples of Christ and brother of John the Evangelist. His adoption as patron saint of Spain extended to the many Spanish conquests in the New World, especially those in Central America.

Haiti　**Blessed Virgin Mary – Our Lady of Perpetual Succour** (27 June): Name derived from a 14th-century icon of Mary, probably painted in Crete, which resided in Venice from the end of the 15th century until taken to Rome about 100 years later, where it was housed, first in the church of St Matthew, then in St Alphonsus' church. Country was dedicated to her under this name in 1942.

Honduras **Blessed Virgin Mary – Our Lady of Suyapa** (3 February): This statue of Mary was found by Indians at Suyapa in 1747, when they broke a journey overnight at the roadside. Declared their patron saint in 1925.

Hungary **Blessed Virgin Mary – Great Queen of Hungary** (8 October): An extension of the devotional idea of Mary as Queen of Heaven. Adopted as patron saint in 1896 to celebrate one thousand years of statehood.

Stephen of Hungary (16 August): Founder and first king of the Christian state of Hungary. Pope Sylvester II sent a crown for his coronation in 1001, which was captured by the United States army during World War II (1939-45), and only returned in 1978.

Iceland **Anskar** (3 February): Bishop of Bremen.

Thorlac (23 December): 12th-century Bishop of Skalholt, one of Iceland's two episcopal sees. Great reformer, founder of a monastery there, and first prelate of Iceland to use excommunication.

India **Blessed Virgin Mary:** Papal approval to a 1950 petition by the country's bishops given the following year.

Francis Xavier (3 December): 16th-century Spanish priest and missionary to the Far East.

Rose of Lima (23 August): 16th-century Peruvian recluse who lived an exemplary life and died at the early age of 31. Patronage of

Peru declared in 1670 and extended to India and Central America a few years later.

Thomas, the Apostle (3 July): One of the twelve disciples of Christ. Dubbed 'Doubting Thomas' because he would not believe Jesus had risen until he could feel the wounds on his body for himself. After the Ascension of Jesus, Thomas travelled to India on missionary work, and was martyred at Madras, where his grave is now marked by a stone cross.

Inner Mongolia
Blessed Virgin Mary – Immaculate Conception (8 December): Feast celebrating Mary's freedom from sin at her conception.

Ireland
Patrick (17 March): British-born saint who brought Christianity to Ireland. As a youth, enslaved for six years by pirates, then returned home, where entered the priesthood. Legend has it that he explained the Trinity by reference to the shamrock, which has become Ireland's national symbol.

Bridget (1 February): In legend, the daughter of a 6th-century cowman from Kildare who became a nun and founded the monastery at Kildare. Also known as St Brigid and St Bride.

Columba (9 June): 6th-century monk who founded several monasteries in Ireland before travelling to the Scottish island of Iona to organize the Church for the Irish in south-west Scotland. Responsible for the consolidation of Christianity in Ireland.

Isle of Man   **Maughold** (27 April): 5th-century Irish pirate sent, by St Patrick, to sea in an open boat without oars, as penance. Landed on Isle of Man, and renounced evil ways in gratitude for deliverance, and eventually became bishop.

Italy   **Francis of Assisi** (12 August): Founder of The Order of Franciscan Friars and renowned animal lover. Born John Bernardone in 1181 and renamed Francesco, 'The French One', by his father. A sometime silk merchant and soldier, he came to the Church, literally, by responding to voices urging him to rebuild a dilapidated place of worship in his home town. Began the still-practised custom of building a crib to celebrate the birth of Jesus.

Catherine of Siena (29 April): 14th-century Italian mystic who spent her early years of devotion caring for the sick. In 1375, attempted to thwart the Great Schism (when a rival to the Pope in Rome set up in opposition in Avignon, in the south of France). Named patron saint of Italy in 1931.

Jamaica   **Blessed Virgin Mary – Feast of the Assumption** (15 August): Feast celebrating Mary's bodily assumption into heaven at her death.

Japan   **Francis Xavier** (3 December): 16th-century Spanish priest and missionary to the Far East.

Martyrs of Japan (6 February): Twenty-six Christians, some Japanese, some European, were persecuted by the ruler Hideyoshi and crucified in Nagasaki in 1597. These included

Paul Miki, a Japanese aristocrat and Jesuit priest, and Peter Baptist, a friar from Avila, Spain, who came as a missionary. All 26 martyrs were canonised in 1862.

Jersey **Helier** (16 July): 6th-century Belgian monk who lived in a closed community with St Marculf in Nanteuil, France, before travelling to Jersey, where he lived in cave just above the town now bearing his name.

Jordan **John the Baptist** (24 June): Herald of the coming of Christ. Born six months before Jesus to a relative of Mary. Began preaching in the desert by the River Jordan, where baptized converts. About the time Jesus began preaching, in the year 30, John was arrested and beheaded on the orders of Herod, at the request of his wife's daughter, Salome.

Lithuania **Casimir of Poland** (4 March): 15th-century prince sent by his father, Casimir IV, to take Hungarian throne by force, but withdrew in face of opposition. Thereafter refused to fight any Christian country, so banished to Dobski, where he led life of austerity and devotion. Died of tuberculosis, aged only 26. Buried in Vilnius, capital of Lithuania.

Cunegund (3 March): 10th-century Princess of Luxembourg who married German Emperor Henry II and founded convent at Kaufungen in Hesse. After Henry's death, she became a Benedictine nun and spent the rest of her life in prayer, also caring for the sick.

146

Luxembourg **Blessed Virgin Mary – Comforter of the Afflicted:** A variation on Mary's title of Our Lady of Consolation, and the name given to an icon in Luxembourg City, venerated since early 17th century, when devotion was fostered by the Jesuits. Mary was proclaimed patron saint in 1678, but not recognised by the Vatican until 1914.

Cunegund (3 March): 10th-century Princess of Luxembourg and Benedictine nun. SEE *Lithuania.*

Willibrord (7 November): English-born Archbishop of Utrecht, Holland, who brought Christianity to Luxembourg in about 720.

Madagascar **Vincent de Paul** (27 September): 16th-century French-born peasant, educated by Franciscan friars, who became confessor to rich and titled families. Also dedicated himself to the poor and sick. Founded a congregation of priests, based at the church of St Lazare in Paris, and an unenclosed Order of women called the Sisters of Charity. His patronage of Madagascar derives from French colonization.

Malta **Paul, the Apostle** (29 June): SEE *Greece*

Mexico **Blessed Virgin Mary – Our Lady of Guadalupe** (12 December): Name of a statue found in the 14th century on a hill outside Guadalupe, Spain, by a shepherd boy, after being guided to it by a vision of Mary herself. Mary also appeared in this guise to a shepherd boy on the hill of Tepayac, outside Mexico

City, in 1531, and told him to instruct the bishop to build a church there. After he had received two refusals, Mary told the boy to gather roses, miraculously growing in the barren earth, in his cloak and take them to the bishop. When the boy let the roses fall from the cloak, an image of Mary was imprinted on the inside. This cloak can still be seen, in Mexico City, and is venerated today.

Netherlands **Willibrord** (7 November): English-born Archbishop of Utrecht who first brought Christianity to the province of Frisia in 690, and then to much of the country.

New Zealand **Blessed Virgin Mary – Our Lady of Help of Christians** (24 May): Patronage arose due to devotion to Mary under this title of early mission-aries from the Society of Mary. SEE *Australia.*

New Caledonia **Blessed Virgin Mary – Feast of the Assumption** (15 August): Feast celebrating Mary's bodily assumption into heaven at her death.

Nicaragua **James the Greater, the Apostle** (25 July): One of the twelve disciples of Christ and brother of John the Evangelist. His adoption as patron saint of Spain extended to Spanish conquests in the New World, especially in Central America.

Nigeria **Blessed Virgin Mary – Queen of Nigeria**: An extension of the devotional idea of Mary as Queen of Heaven. Confirmed as patron saint in 1961.

Norway   **Olaf** (29 July): King of Norway, from 1016-1029, who brought Christianity to the country by force. This was met with rebellion, leading to exile in 1029 and death at battle of Stiklestad in 1030, while attempting to regain throne.

Magnus of Orkney (16 April): 11th-century Earl of Orkney, originally a pirate before conversion to Christianity. Taken prisoner by Magnus Barefoot, King of Norway, but refused to join in raids on Britain. Escaped to the court of Malcolm III of Scotland, returning home only when Magnus Barefoot died. Murdered in 1116, on the orders of his cousin, Haakon, with whom he ruled Orkney. Said to have appeared to Robert the Bruce on the eve of the Battle of Bannockburn in 1314, promising him victory.

Orkneys   **Magnus of Orkney** (16 April): 11th-century Earl of Orkney. SEE *Norway*.

Outer Mongolia   **Francis Xavier** (3 December): 16th-century Spanish priest and missionary to the Far East.

Pakistan   **Thomas, the Apostle** (3 July): SEE *India*.

Francis Xavier (3 December): 16th-century Spanish priest and missionary to the Far East.

Papua NG   **Michael, the Archangel** (29 September): SEE *Germany*.

Paraguay   **Blessed Virgin Mary – Feast of the Assumption** (15 August): Feast celebrating Mary's bodily assumption into heaven at her death. Capital city, Asunción, is named after the Feast in recognition of the foundation of the first episcopal see, after conquest in 1547.

Philippines **Blessed Virgin Mary – Immaculate Conception** (8 December): Feast celebrating Mary's freedom from sin at her conception.

Peru **Joseph** (19 March): Husband of Mary, mother of Jesus.

Rose of Lima (23 August): First saint of the American continent. Born into a 16th-century Spanish family in Lima, Peru. Took Holy Orders and lived an exemplary life until early death, at the age of 31, in 1617. Declared patron saint of Peru in 1670 by Pope Clement X.

Turibius of Mogroveio (23 March): 16th-century Spanish professor who became chief judge of the Inquisition. Sent to Peru in 1581 to become Archbishop of Lima. Tightened up discipline in the Christian community and founded many new churches and hospitals. Canonised in 1726.

Poland **Blessed Virgin Mary – Queen of Poland** (3 May): Extension of the devotional idea of Mary as Queen of Heaven. Declared patron saint under this title by the 17th-century king, John Casimir, after successful defence of a shrine at Czestochowa, during war with Sweden, was attributed to intercession from Mary.

Adalbert of Prague (23 April): First native bishop of Prague. SEE *Czech Republic.*

Stanislaus (11 April): 11th-century Polish nobleman turned priest who became Bishop of Cracow. Zealous reformer of the Polish Church and generous benefactor of the poor. Quarrel with the violent and unjust King Boleslaus II led to his murder, in 1079, at the hands of the King himself, in a chapel outside the town.

Portugal

Blessed Virgin Mary – The Assumption (15 August): Feast celebrating Mary's Assumption into heaven at her death.

Antony of Padua (13 June): 12th-century Portuguese knight who became a monk and crossed the Straits of Gibraltar to evangelize among the Moors. Illness forced him to return, but was shipwrecked and landed in Sicily. Travelled as far as Assisi where talents as a preacher were discovered. Also spent many years ministering to the poor.

George (23 April): 4th-century soldier-saint.

Francis Borgia (10 October): 16th-century Spanish Duke and provincial ruler who became a Jesuit priest on the death of his wife. First appointed Commissary of Spain and Portugal to oversee Jesuit activity. Then became General of Jesuits, in 1561, when called to Rome. Founded many houses in Europe and initiated missionary work on the American continent.

Puerto Rico

Blessed Virgin Mary – Our Lady of Divine Providence: Assigned patron saint by Pope

Paul VI in 1969 because of many centuries' devotion to Mary under this title.

Russia   **Joseph** (19 March): Husband of Mary, the mother of Jesus.

Andrew, the Apostle (30 November): SEE *Scotland.*

Basil the Great (2 January): 4th-century Bishop of Caesarea, Asia Minor, renowned for his learning, and as a defender Christian doctrine and opposer of heresies. Responsible for many writings, including several on monastic law, still followed in Greek and Russian Orthodox Churches.

Nicholas of Bari (6 December): 4th-century Bishop of Myra, Turkey, with a reputation for being a wonder-worker. Legend credits him with a number of acts of mercy which have linked him to several professions and groups. Widely venerated after his death, especially in the Eastern Church and in the Netherlands.

Sardinia   **Ephysus** (15 January): 4th-century martyr executed during persecutions of Roman Emperor Diocletian.

Maurice (22 September): 3rd-century Egyptian soldier.

Scotland   **Andrew, the Apostle** (30 November): Fisherman brother of Simon Peter, called to follow Christ as one of the twelve apostles. He is specially mentioned for his share in feeding the 5,000 Greeks who came to see Jesus, as

recounted in St John's Gospel. The where-
abouts of his missionary work and death, in
about the year 60, are unknown, but legend has
it that his relics were taken to Scotland by St
Rule in the 8th century. Andrew is depicted in
art with the saltire (diagonal) cross, which is
incorporated in the Union Flag of the United
Kingdom to represent Scotland.

Andrew Avellino (10 November): 16th-
century Neapolitan priest, reformer of lapsed
religious houses, founder of other houses all
over Italy, and vigorous opponent of the
Reformation.

Sicily

Vitus (15 June): Son of a 4th-century pagan
Sicilian senator of the Roman Empire. Conversion to Christianity led to his arrest, but he
escaped and fled to Rome, where caught up in
the persecutions of the Emperor Diocletian and
executed, together with his nurse, Crescentia,
and tutor, Modestus.

Rosalia of Palermo (4 September): 12th-
century daughter of a wealthy Sicilian family
who became a religious recluse, living in a cave
near Bavona, before moving permanently to a
grotto in Mount Pellegrino, near Palermo. Her
relics lay there, undiscovered, until 1624.

Slovak
Republic

Blessed Virgin Mary – Our Lady of Sorrows
(15 September): The name derives from Mary's
distress at the crucifixion of her son, Jesus
Christ. Devotion to Mary on this date stems
from the Feast of the Triumph of the Cross,
celebrated in the Middle Ages at the start of the

Monastic Lent, which continued up until Easter, with a break for Christmas.

Solomon Is   **Maurice** (22 September): Third-century Egyptian soldier.

S. Vietnam   **Joseph** (19 March): Husband of Mary, mother of Jesus.

Southern Africa   **Blessed Virgin Mary – The Assumption** (15 August): Feast Day of Mary's bodily assumption into Heaven after her death.

Spain   **Blessed Virgin Mary – Immaculate Conception** (8 December): Feast celebrating Mary's freedom from sin at her conception.

James the Greater, the Apostle (25 July): One of the twelve disciples of Christ and brother of John the Evangelist. He witnessed the Transfiguration of Christ and the Agony in the Garden of Gethsemane. First Apostle to be martyred, in Jerusalem in 44, under Herod Agrippa, as recorded in the *Acts of the Apostles*. Mediaeval legends recount that he preached in Spain and that his body was transported to the shrine of Santiago de Compostela after his death. This shrine was enormously popular in the Middle Ages, and James became the focus for the defence of Christianity against the Moors, who occupied southern Spain until they were expelled in 15th century. Adoption as patron saint of Spain extended to Spanish conquests in New World, especially Central America.

Sri Lanka   **Blessed Virgin Mary – The Immaculate 'Our Lady of Lanka':** Devotion to Mary was fostered in the 19th century by missionaries of the Oblate of Mary Immaculate. The Archbishop of the capital, Colombo, dedicated the island, then known as Ceylon, to Mary as Our Lady of Lanka in 1947, as the people believed it was her intercession that saved the island from invasion by the Japanese in World War II.

Sweden   **Bridget (23 July):** The daughter of a 14th-century Swedish provincial governor, who became a nun on the death of her husband in 1343, and founded a monastery at Vadstena, on Lake Vattern. Went to Rome for Papal approval of her Order in 1349, but did not return to Sweden. Performed numerous good works among Roman poor until her death in 1373.

Eric the Martyr (18 May): 12th-century King of Sweden who established Christianity there and commissioned the building of Sweden's first large church, at Uppsala. He vanquished invading pagan Finns and sent the English bishop, Henry, to evangelize there. Murdered in 1161 by a band of rebel Swedes and soldiers of hostile King of Denmark, while hearing Mass.

Switzerland   **Nicholas von Flue (21 March, but 25 September in Switzerland):** Born in 1417, in Flueli. Never ordained, but became a member of a lay association, the Friends of God, and retired as a hermit in nearby Ranft for the last

20 years of his life. Often consulted by statesmen and ordinary people, and instrumental in the inclusion of the two states of Fribourg and Soleure in the newly formed confederation of Switzerland, which won its independence from Burgundy in 1485. Died in 1487 and canonised in 1669.

Tanzania	**Blessed Virgin Mary – Immaculate Conception** (8 December): Feast celebrating Mary's freedom from sin at her conception.
Turkey	**John the Evangelist, the Apostle** (27 December): One of the twelve who followed Christ, and present at the Transfiguration. Also one of the Apostles who slept during Christ's Agony in the Garden of Gethsemane. Took Mary as his adopted mother, as directed by Christ and, after the Resurrection, suffered persecution under the Roman Emperor Domitian. Then travelled to Ephesus, in what is now Turkey, to evangelize. Author of the fourth New Testament Gospel and the three *Epistles of John*.
United States of America	**Blessed Virgin Mary – Immaculate Conception** (8 December): Feast celebrating Mary's freedom from sin at her conception.
Uruguay	**Blessed Virgin Mary – Our Lady of Thirty-Three** (19 April): Named after 33 exiles who returned in 1825 to fight for independence from Brazil. Set up headquarters in the city of Florida, where there was a shrine to Our Lady of Lujan. The success of the rising, leading to signing of the Declaration of Independence,

was attributed to intercession from Mary, and she was confirmed as patron saint, under the title of Our Lady of Thirty-Three, in 1962.

Blessed Virgin Mary – Our Lady of Lujan (Saturday before the fourth Sunday after Easter): Name derives from a 17th-century shrine at Lujan, Argentina.

Philip and James, the Apostles (3 May): Two of the twelve disciples of Christ. Philip was a Galilean and a follower of John the Baptist before being called by Jesus. James was the second apostle of that name, usually called 'James the Less', who is sometimes identified as the author of the *Epistle of St. James*. He was martyred in the year 62.

Venezuela   **Blessed Virgin Mary – Our Lady of Coromoto** (11 September): The Cospes Indians, who lived near the town of Guanare, claimed their conversion to Christianity was at the insistence of Mary, who appeared to their chief in 1651 and 1652. After establishing a missionary village at Coromoto, the chief fell into his old ways. Mary appeared again, to rebuke him, and he attacked the apparition. The vision instantly disappeared, leaving him holding a statue of Mary. She was declared patron saint under this title in 1942.

Wales   **David** (1 March): The only Welsh saint to be canonised. A 6th-century monk and bishop, David founded at least ten monasteries, including Glastonbury, and Menevia, in south-west Wales, now called St David's. His relics rest in the cathedral there. Claimed as patron saint since 12th century.

West Indies **Gertrude of Helfta** (16 November): 13th-century nun from Helfta in Saxony, southern Germany, who underwent several mystic experiences including visions of Christ, as recorded in her writings. Her name appears in the Roman martyrology of 1677, but she has never been canonised.

Zaire **Blessed Virgin Mary – Immaculate Conception** (8 December): Feast celebrating Mary's freedom from sin at her conception.

A Calendar of
Saints' Days

MOST diaries note a few Saints' Days, together with information about the phases of the moon and national holidays. You will probably be able to count the number of such entries on one hand but, as you will see from our listing, every day is in fact a Feast Day. Several hundred saints are listed here, including all those featured elsewhere in this book, indicated in **bold type**.

Some Feast Days are marked by a celebration. The Church may direct a Mass to be said, for example, if the saint is of sufficient importance; perhaps a carnival is held, or a fair, or a symbol worn to show recognition of the day. But, other than this, no rules are laid down. Instead, believers are free to express devotion in their own, individual way. Wellknown saints are celebrated universally, but some listed here may only be venerated and have their Feast Day marked in a single village.

JANUARY

1 Abbot Clarus; Blessed Virgin Mary; Odilo; Peter of Atroa
2 Caspar del Bufalo; Basil the Great; Gregory of Nazianzus; Munchin
3 Genevieve
4 Elizabeth Bayley Seton; Roger of Ellant
5 John Neumann; Simon Stylites
6 John de Ribera; Peter of Canterbury
7 Brannoc; Raymund of Penafort; Lucian
8 Thorfinn; Nathalan; Wulsin
9 Adrian of Canterbury; Berhtwald; Basilissa and Julian
10 Peter Orseolo; Paul the Hermit; Dermot
11 Theodosius the Cenobiarch
12 Benedict Biscop; Ailred; Salvius
13 Hilary; Kentigern (Mungo)
14 Sabas; Felix of Nola
15 Ita; Ceolwulf; Ephysus
16 Honoratus of Arles; Sigebert; Henry of Coquet Island
17 Antony of Egypt (the Abbot); Mildgyth; Sulpicius
18 Deicolus; Prisca; Ulfrid
19 Wulfstan; Canute; Henry of Finland
20 Sebastian; Fabian; Euthymius the Great
21 Meinrad; Agnes
22 Vincent of Saragossa; Anastatius
23 John the Almsgiver; Emerentiana
24 Francis of Sales; Babylas; Cadoc
25 Paul (conversion of); Dwyn; Praejectus
26 Timothy and Titus; Eystein; Conan; Paula; Bathild
27 Angela Merici; Julian of Le Mans; Avitus; Devota
28 Thomas Aquinas; John the Sage
29 Gildas the Wise; Julian the Hospitaller
30 Hyacintha Mariscotti
31 John Bosco; Maedoc of Ferns

FEBRUARY

1 Bridget of Ireland; Henry Morse; Seiriol
2 Joan de Lestonnac
3 Blaise; Anskar; Laurence of Canterbury; Mary, Our Lady of Suyapa
4 Gilbert of Sempringham; John de Britto
5 Agatha; Adelaide of Bellich
6 Amand; Paul Miki and Companions (Martyrs of Japan); Dorothy
7 Luke the Younger; Richard; Romuld
8 Jerome Emiliani; Cuthman; Elfleda
9 Apollonia; Teilo
10 Scholastica; Trumwine
11 Caedmon; Gregory II; Benedict of Aniane
12 Ethilwald; Meletius
13 Catherine dei Ricci; Ermingild; Huna
14 Valentine; Cyril and Methodius; Zeno of Rome
15 Sigfrid of Växjö
16 Julian
17 Finan of Lindisfarne; Fintan of Clonenagh; 7 Servite Founders
18 Theotonius; Colman of Lindisfarne
19 Boniface of Lausanne
20 Wulfric
21 Peter Damian; Fructuosus
22 Margaret of Cortona
23 Polycarp; Jurmin; Milburga
24 Matthias; Praetextatus
25 Tarasius; Ethelbert of Kent; Walburga
26 Alexander of Alexandria
27 Gabriel Possenti; Alnoth; Leander; Herefrith
28 Oswald of Worcester; Romanus
29 John Cassian

MARCH

1 **David of Wales**; Swithbert
2 Chad; Joavan
3 **Cunegund**; Marinus
4 **Adrian the Martyr**; **Casimir of Poland**
5 John Joseph of the Cross; Ciaran of Saighir
6 Colette; Baldred and Bilfrith;
7 Drausius; Perpetua and Felicitas
8 John of God; Felix of Dunwich
9 **Dominic Savio, Frances of Rome**; Constantine; Gregory of Nyssa
10 Kessog; John Ogilvie
11 Oengus
12 **Gregory the Great**; Theophanes the Chronicler; Paul Aurelian
13 Gerald of Mayo; Mochoemoc; Euphrasia
14 Leobinus
15 **Louise de Marillac**; Longinus; Zacharias
16 Abraham Kidunaia; Finan Lobur; Gregory of Armenia
17 **Patrick**; **Joseph of Arimathea**; **Gertrude of Nivelles**
18 Cyril of Jerusalem; Edward the Martyr; Finan of Aberdeen
19 **Joseph**; Alcmund
20 Cuthbert; Herbert of Derwentwater; Wulfram
21 **Nicholas of Flue**; Enda
22 Nicholas Owen
23 Turibius of Mogroveio; Gwinear
24 Catherine of Sweden; Irenaeus of Sirmium; Hildelith; Macartan
25 Dismas; Lucy Filippini; **Blessed Virgin Mary – The Annunciation**
26 William of Norwich; Braulio; Liudger
27 John of Egypt; Ruper of Salzburg
28 Alkelda of Middleham; Tutilo
29 Gwynllyw and Gwladys
30 Zosimus of Syracuse; John Climacus; Osburga
31 Guy of Pomposa

APRIL

1 Hugh of Grenoble; Gilbert of Caithness; Agilbert; Tewdric; Walaric
2 **Francis of Paola**; Mary of Egypt
3 Pancras of Taormina; Richard of Wyche; Agape, Irene & Chione
4 Isidore of Seville; Ambrose
5 Vincent Ferrer; Derfel
6 Elstan; William of Eskilsoë
7 **John Baptist de la Salle**; Celsus; Finan Cam
8 Julia Billiart
9 Waldetrudis; Madrun
10 Hedda of Peterborough; Fulbert
11 **Stanislaus of Crakow**; Guthlac
12 Zeno of Verona; Alferius
13 Hermenegild; Pope Martin I; Carpus, Papylus and Agathonice
14 Caradoc; Bénezet
15 Hunna; Paternus of Wales; Basilissa and Anastasia
16 **Mary Bernarda (Bernadette)**; **Magnus of Orkney**; **Benedict Joseph Labre**
17 Donnan; Stephen Harding
18 Galdinus; Laserian
19 Alphege of Canterbury; Pope Leo IX
20 Caedwalla; Agnes of Montepulciano
21 Anselm; Beuno; Ethelwald; Maelrubba
22 Theodore of Sykeon
23 **George**; Adalbert of Prague
24 Fidelis of Sigmaringen; Egbert; Ives; Mellitus
25 **Mark the Evangelist**
26 Cletus; Riquier; Mary, Motherhood of Good Counsel
27 **Maughold**; Zita
28 Louis de Montfort; Vitalis; Peter Chanel
29 **Catherine of Siena**; Hugh of Cluny; Peter the Martyr
30 Erkenwald; Pope Pius V

MAY

1 Peregrine Laziosi; Marculf; Asaph
2 Athanasius; Gennys
3 Holy Cross; Philip and James; Mary – Queen of Poland
4 Godehard
5 Hilary; Hydroc
6 Marian and James; Petronax
7 John of Beverley
8 Peter of Tarantaise; Indract; Odger
9 Pachomius
10 Cathal; Antoninus of Florence
11 Gengulf; Francis de Girolamo; Congall, Tudy; Mary the Immaculate 'Aparecida'
12 Germanus of Constantinople; Pancras of Rome
13 Robert Bellarmine; John the Silent
14 Matthias; Gemma Galgani
15 Isidore the Farmer; Dympna
16 Honoratus of Amiens; Ubald of Gubbio; John Nepomucen; Brendan
17 Paschal Baylon; Madron
18 Elgiva; Pope John I; Eric of Sweden
19 Ivo of Kermartin; Dunstan; Peter Celestine
20 Bernardino of Siena; Ethelbert of East Anglia
21 Andrew Bobola; Collen; Godric
22 Rita of Cascia; Helen of Carnarfon; Julia
23 William of Rochester; John Baptist Rossi
24 Vincent of Lérins; David of Scotland; Mary, Our Lady of Help of Christians
25 Madalein Sophie Barat; Pope Gregory VII; Urban; Zenobius
26 Augustine of Canterbury; Philip Neri
27 Bede; Julius the Veteran
28 Bernard of Aosta; Germanus of Paris
29 Bona; William of Toulouse
30 Ferdinand III of Castile; Hubert; Joan of Arc
31 Mechtildis of Edelstetten; Blessed Virgin Mary – The Visitation

JUNE

1 Inigo; Nicomedes; Gwen of Britanny; Justin
2 Erasmus (Elmo); Marcellinus and Peter; Oda
3 Charles Lwanga and Companions; Genesius of Clermont; Kevin
4 Francis Caracciolo; Edfrith; Ninnoc; Petroc
5 Boniface
6 Norbert; Primus and Felician
7 Robert of Newminster
8 William of York; Medard
9 Our Lady of Grace; Ephraem; Columba
10 Ithamar
11 Barnabas
12 Basilides; Pope Leo II; John of Sahagun; Eskil; Odulf
13 Antony of Padua
14 Dogmael; Methodius
15 Vitus; Trillo; Germaine of Pibrac
16 John Francis Regis; Lutgardis; Cyricus; Ismael
17 Teresa and Sanchia of Portugal; Botolph
18 Mark and Marcellian; Elizabeth of Schönau; Adrian of Bordeaux
19 Juliana Falconieri; Gervase and Protase; Romuald
20 Alban; Govan; Silverius
21 Aloysius Gonzaga; Leufred
22 John Fisher; Thomas More; Paulinus of Nola
23 Cyneburg; Etheldreda
24 John the Baptist; Bartholomew of Farne
25 Adalbert of Egmond; William of Vercelli
26 John and Paul; Salvius; Anthelm
27 Cyril of Alexandria; Zoilus; Mary, Our Lady of Perpetual Succour
28 Irenaeus of Lyons; Austell
29 Peter the Apostle; Paul of Tarsus; Elwin; Judith and Salome
30 Martyrs of Rome

162

JULY

1 Oliver Plunket; Julius and Aaron
2 Blessed Virgin Mary; Otto; Processus and Martinian
3 Germanus of Man; **Thomas the Apostle**
4 **Martin of Tours**; Elizabeth of Portugal
5 Athanasius the Athonite; Modwenna; Morwenna; Zacaria
6 Maria Goretti; Newlyx; Sexburga
7 Palladius; Hedda of Winchester
8 Grimbald; Killian; Withburga
9 Nicholas Pieck and Companions
10 Alexander; Seven Brothers
11 **Benedict**; Drostan; Thurketyl
12 John Gualbert; **Veronica**
13 Mildred; Silas
14 **Camillus de Lellis**; Boniface of Savoy; Phocas of Sinope
15 Bonaventure; David of Sweden; Swithun, Vladimir
16 Fulrad; **Helier**; Plechtelm; **Mary, Our Lady of Mount Carmel**
17 Clement of Okhrida and Companions; Alexis
18 Bruno of Segni; Edburga of Bicester
19 Macrina the Younger
20 **Margaret of Antioch** (suppressed);Vulmar; Wilgefortis
21 Laurence of Brindisi; Praxedes; Victor
22 Mary Magdalene; Wandrille; Philip Evans and John Lloyd
23 **Bridget of Sweden**; Apollinarius
24 Christina the Astonishing; Boris and Gleb; Wulfhad; Ruffin
25 **Christopher; James the Greater**
26 Bartholomea Capitanio; Joachim; **Anne**
27 **Pantaleon**; Seven Sleepers
28 Samson of Dol; Botvid
29 **Martha; Olaf of Norway**; Lupus; Simplicius; Sullian
30 Abdon and Sennen; Peter Chrysologus
31 Ignatius Loyola; Germanus of Auxerre; Neot

AUGUST

1 Peter Julian Eymard; Alphonsus; Ethelwold; Kyned; Macabees
2 Etheldritha; Thomas of Hales; Eusebius; **Mary, Our Lady of the Angels**
3 Walthen; Manaccus
4 **Sithney**; Molua; John Vianney
5 Cassyon; Oswald of Northumbria; Addai and Mari
6 Hormisdas; Sixtus; **Salvador del Mundo**
7 Cajetan
8 **Cyriacus (with Largus)**; Dominic; Lide
9 **Emygdius**; Romanus
10 **Laurence**; Bettelin
11 **Clare**; Blane; Tiburtius and Susanna
12 Porcarius and Companions; Jambert; Murtagh
13 **Cassian of Imola**; Hippolytus; Maximus the Confessor
14 Maximillian Kolbe; Marcellus
15 **Blessed Virgin Mary – The Assumption**; Arnulf; Tarsicius
16 Roch; **Stephen of Hungary**
17 Clare of Montefalco
18 Helen; Agapitus
19 Credan; John Eudes; Mochta
20 **Bernard of Clairvaux**; Oswin
21 Pope Pius X
22 Sigfrid of Wearmouth; Alexander; Arnulf; **The Most Pure Heart of Mary**
23 Rose of Lima; Philip Benizi
24 Audoenus; Bartholomew
25 **Genesius; Louis IX of France**; Joseph Calasanz
26 **Teresa of Jornet e Ibars**; Ninian Bregwine; Elizabeth Bichier
27 Caesarius of Arles; Decuman
28 Augustine of Hippo; Hermes
29 **John the Baptist**; Medericus; Edwold; Sebbi
30 Pammachius; Felix and Adauctus; Rumon
31 **Raymund Nonnatus**; Aidan of Lindisfarne

SEPTEMBER

1 Fiacre; Giles; Drithelm
2 William of Roskilde
3 Basilissa the Martyr; Macansius
4 Rose of Viterbo; Ultan; Rosalia of Palermo
5 Bertin; Laurence of Giustiniani
6 Magnus of Fussen; Bega
7 Cloud; Evurtius; Tilbert
8 Adrian Nicomedia; Corbinian; Kinemark; Blessed Virgin Mary
9 Peter Claver; Ciaran of Clonmacnoise; Gorgonius; Wulfhilda
10 Nicholas of Tolentino; Finian of Moville; Frithestan
11 Paphnutius; Protus and Hyacinth; Deiniol; Mary – Our Lady of Coromoto
12 Ailbe; Guy of Anderlecht
13 John Chrysostom
14 Holy Cross; Notburga
15 Adam of Caithness; Catherine of Genoa; Blessed Virgin Mary – Our Lady of Sorrows
16 Cornelius; Cyprian; Edith
17 Hildegard; Lambert
18 Joseph of Cupertino
19 Emily de Rodat; Januarius; Theodore of Canterbury
20 Vincent Madelgarius
21 Matthew; Michael of Chernigov and Theodore
22 Maurice; Thomas of Villanova; Laudus
23 Adamnan of Iona; Thecla
24 Robert of Knaresborough; Gerard of Csanad; Mary, Our Lady of Mercy
25 Albert of Jerusalem; Ceolfrith; Cadoc; Firmin; Finbar; Sergius
26 Cosmas and Damian; Teresa Couderc; Cyprian and Justina
27 Vincent de Paul; Barry; Florentius
28 Bernardino of Feltres; Wenceslaus of Bohemia; Lioba
29 Archangels Gabriel, Michael and Raphael
30 Jerome; Honorius; Tancred; Torthred and Tova

OCTOBER

1 Thérèse of Lisieux; Mylor
2 Thomas of Hereford; The Guardian Angels; Leger
3 Hewalds; Thomas Cantalupe
4 Francis of Assisi
5 Maurus and Placid; Flora of Beaulieu
6 Bruno; Faith
7 Helen of Cornwall; Osith
8 Iwi; Keyne; Triduana; Mary, Great Queen of Hungary
9 Denis, Bishop of Paris; Louis Betrand; John Leonardi
10 Francis Borgia; Geron
11 Canice; Mary Soledad; Peter of Alcantara
12 Wilfrid; Edwin
13 Edward the Confessor; Comgan; Gerald of Aurillac; Coloman
14 Pope Calixtus I; Burchard, Manacca and Selavan
15 Tecla; Teresa of Avila
16 Gall; Gerald Majella
17 Ignatius of Antioch; Margaret-Mary Alacoque
18 Luke; John of Bridlington; Gwen of Cornwall
19 Paul of the Cross; Martyrs of North America
20 Bertilla Boscardin; Acca
21 Hilarion; Tuda; Ursula
22 Donatus; Mellon; Philip and Companions
23 John of Capistrano; Ethelfleda
24 Antony Claret; Maglorius; Felix of Thibiuca
25 Crispin and Crispinian; 40 Martyrs of England & Wales; Robert Southwell
26 Bean; Cedd; Eata
27 Odran; Frumentius
28 Simon and Jude; Salvius
29 Colman of Kilmacduagh; Theuderius; Merewenna
30 Alphonsus Rodriguez; Marcellus the Centurion
31 All Souls; Begu; Erc; Foillan; Quentin; Wolfgang

NOVEMBER

1 All Saints; Benignus; Cadfan; Dingad; Gwythian; Vigor
2 Marcian
3 Martin de Porres; Pirminus; Clydog; Malachy; Rumwold; Wulgan
4 Charles Borromeo; Birstan; Clether; Florian
5 Bertilla of Chelles; Kea; Zachary and Elizabeth
6 Illtud; Leonard; Melaine; Mennas; Winnoc
7 Congar; Willibrord
8 Godfrey; Cybi; 4 Crowned Martyrs; Tysilio; Gerardin
9 Benignus; Theodore
10 Andrew Avellino; Pope Leo the Great; Justus; Aed
11 Martin of Tours; Theodore the Studite
12 Josaphat; Cadwaladr; Lebuin; Machar
13 Homobonus; Abbo; Stanislaus Kotska
14 Dyfrig; Laurence O'Toole; Modan
15 Leopold; Albert the Great; Fintan of Rheinau; Malo
16 Edmund of Abingdon; Margaret of Scotland; Gertrude of Helfta
17 Elizabeth of Hungary; Gregory of Tours; Hilda; Hugh of Lincoln
18 Mabin; Mawes; Odilo of Cluny; Mary, Our Lady of Chiquinquira
19 Nerses I; Ermenburga; Ronan
20 Edmund the Martyr
21 Albert of Louvain; Condedus; Mary, Our Lady of Peace
22 Cecilia; Philemon and Apphia
23 Clement; Columbanus
24 Chrysogonus; Colman of Cloyne; Enfleda; Minver
25 Catherine of Alexandria; Moses of Rome
26 Silvester Gozzolini
27 Virgil; Congar; Fergus
28 Juthwara; Catherine Labouré
29 Brendan of Birr; Radbod
30 Andrew; Cuthbert Mayne

DECEMBER

1 Edmund Campion; Eloi; Tudwal
2 Chromatius
3 Francis Xavier; Birinus
4 Barbara; John Damascene; Osmund
5 Sabas; Christian of Markyate; Justinian; Crispina
6 Nicholas of Bari
7 Ambrose; Diuma
8 Romaric; Blessed Virgin Mary –The Immaculate Conception; Budoc
9 Peter Fourier; Wolfeius
10 Pope Gregory III; Eulalia
11 Damasus; Gentian; Daniel the Stylite
12 Jane Frances de Chantal; Finnian of Clonard; Mary, Our Lady of Guadalupe
13 Lucy; Judoc; Edburga of Minster; Odilia
14 John of the Cross; Venantius; Fortunatus; Hybald; Nicasius
15 Mary di Rosa; Offa of Essex
16 Adelaide; Bean
17 Lazarus of Bethany; Sturmi
18 Flannan; Mawnan; Samthann; Winnibald
19 Pope Anastasius I
20 Dominic of Silos
21 Thomas the Apostle; Peter Canisius; Beornwald of Bampton
22 Frances Xavier Cabrini; Chaeremon and Ischyrion
23 John of Kanti; Frithebert; Thorlac
24 Mochua; Irmina and Adela
25 Anastasia the Martyr
26 Stephen; Tathai
27 John the Evangelist; Theodore and Theophanes
28 The Holy Innocents; Antony of Lérins
29 Thomas Becket of Canterbury; Evrault
30 Egwin
31 Pope Silvester I

INDEX TO PRINCIPAL ENTRIES

INDEX

SELECT BIBLIOGRAPHY

- *Butler's Lives of the Saints, Volumes I-IV* (Burns & Oates, 1982)
- *Butler's Lives of the Saints, Concise Edition*, edited by Michael Walsh (Burns & Oates, 1985)
- *Butler's Lives of the Patron Saints*, edited by Michael Walsh (Burns & Oates, 1987)
- *Oxford Dictionary of Saints* by David Hugh Farmer (Oxford University Press, 1992)
- *Chambers Encyclopedic Guides: Saints* by Alison Jones (Chambers, 1992)
- *Penguin Dictionary of Saints*, edited by Donald Attwater (Penguin, 1987)
- *A Calendar of Saints* by Vincent Cronin (Darton, Longman & Todd, 1963)
- *Book of Saints* by The Benedictine Monks of St Augustine's, Ramsgate, Kent (A & C Black, 1989)
- *Yearbook of Saints* by Christine Chandler (Mowbray, 1981)
- *Saints of Patronage and Invocation* by Michael Gibson (Avon County Library, 1982)
- *Illustrated History of Saints and Symbols* by Olwen Reed (Spurbooks, 1978)